MIRACLES in *Natoma's* KITCHEN

Healthy Downhome Cooking

This highly practical author shows you
the "how" of cooking low-fat at its best!

PUBLISHED BY

ALPHA LIFESPAN

EVANSVILLE, INDIANA

First Printing - October, 1995
Second Printing - November, 1995

In view of the complex, individual, and specific nature of health and fitness problems, this book is not intended to replace professional medical advice. The author and publisher expressly disclaim responsibility for any liability loss or risk, personal or otherwise which is incurred as a consequence, directly or indirectly, of the use and application of any of the contents of this book.

ISBN: 1-886246-04-1

A LOWFAT CONNECTION ® BOOK

CREDITS: The Wimmer Companies for their vital role in printing this book.
Photo Credits: Bill Smith, Newburgh, IN, for his excellent product photos.

A NOTE FROM THE AUTHOR

Again, this book is written for the person, the ordinary person, wanting to lose weight with plain, ordinary downhome style cooking.

Or, you may be a person trying to lower your cholesterol level, or blood pressure. Naturally, this type of advice would normally come from your physician.

Like last year's low-fat cookbook, these new recipes have been kept as simple as possible so that you can go to your own local grocer and shop as a normal person.

I've included "Recipes for all occasions" which has the special holiday recipes from my other book due to popular request. These recipes should make your low fat journey much easier.

As you know, the holidays are special times. They're also critical times for people with weight loss concerns. So, here's some help for you.

DEDICATION

Bill, Sherri, and Terri,

our adult children,

each of which are special in their own way.

mom and dad, Fred & Dorothy Belcher (n.r.)

dad, W. F. Riley Sr. and Lucille (f.r.)

stepmother Gloria Smith (f.r.)

May the Lord bless their lives and families

Frank Riley & Natoma Riley

DISCLAIMER PAGE

The author and publisher of this book are not physicians and are not licensed to give medical advice. The information in this book has been collected for the convenience of the reader. The fat values for prepared foods are subject to change and might currently vary from listings herein, which are based on research conducted in the summer, 1995.

Such information does not constitute a recommendation or endorsement of any individual, institution or product, nor is it intended as a substitute for personalized consultation with your physician. The authors and publisher disclaim any liability arising directly or indirectly from the use of this book.

The nutritional analysis was done for us by M.E.P. Healthcare, Evansville, IN using NutriMax Software, ProSoft Technologies.

Neither the authors, Alpha LifeSpan, nor Low Fat Connection (LFC) CLAIM THAT THESE RECIPES ARE ORIGINAL. "I have taken recipes from many sources and reduced them down to the lowest fats as possible, but maintaining their good taste." (N.R.)

For more information, write:
Alpha LifeSpan, 4701 Theater Drive, Evansville, IN 47715 or, call 812-473-1052

ACKNOWLEDGMENTS

There are so many people who should be thanked for helping us in this project.

A big, big thanks to Evelyn Smith, a co-worker with "a heart of gold". She displayed a willingness to go above and beyond her "duty" that amazed us at LFC.

Stephanie Koring worked very hard with us entering all the computer data entry work along with her regular office work duties.

Debbie Denton and Mary Ellen Posthauer, R.D., of M.E.P. Healthcare Dietary Services, Inc. gave their time and efforts in an exceptional way to provide us with a sound nutritional analysis of our recipes.

Gloria Smith deserves a special thanks. She read the first draft of the recipes and helped us in corrections. Thanks.

Jeff and Judy Norrington, friends and professional associates also contributed immensely to our efforts. Gary Ritchel, president of Creative Press, Inc. encouraged us and gave invaluable suggestions in the early stages of the project too.

And of course the entire staff at The Wimmer Companies, Inc. has nurtured and given us so much of their time and expertise. The office staff has been great. I especially want to single out Glen Wimmer, Christine Clarke, and Sheila Thomas for their hard work.

Last, but not least, we thank the little flock of the Mt. Vernon Church of Christ for allowing Frank the time and effort to serve in all of this as a constant source of encouragement instead of complaint.

PREFACE

Last summer, when I wrote and published my ***Natoma's Low Fat Home-Style Cooking*** I had no idea where the book would go in terms of sales and outreach. Listening to my "fatbusters" at LFC in early 1994 and prompted by their asking me to put my recipes together into a book form, I embarked on a journey.

Now, some 17,000 books later in print and experiencing the widespread support of many people. This support includes women who were tired of cookbooks that:

A. could hardly be understood by ingredients and terms confusing to consumers, and

B. created repeated frustration to consumers because as they went to their local grocery they often could not find many of the foods listed in these books.

But their experiences were my experiences. Years earlier as I lost my 110 pounds in 14 months I too became frustrated, disappointed, and confused with the marketplace.

The marketplace has changed in this last year. But not enough.

Natoma Riley
August, 1995

TABLE OF CONTENTS

INTRODUCTION

Early last year, hardly anyone said much about low fat cooking and its relationship with nutrition and weight loss. Then, somewhere down the line, America went to bed one night and woke up “lowfat”!
It’s amazing. In February, 1994, when I started my company “The Low Fat Connection” little low-fat information was available for the consumer. Not so today. Its everywhere.

People are coming around.
Low fat is definitely in.
In fact, earlier this year one group The Center for Science in the Public Interest targeted two West Virginia towns to persuade people to switch from whole or 2% milk to skim or 1% milk. Result? Sales of skim and !% milk doubled from January to April, rising from 18% to 37% of all milk sold. (*USA Today,* 1D, July 13, 1995)

That's not all. Look at the themes you see in book titles and other sources. Think about it.

Do you want a taste of health? Want freedom from fat?
Need a "Fat Attack" plan?
And, did you know that fat is a feminist issue too?
Do you know God's answer to fat? Lose it!

Thin is In! Somewhere down the line we changed. We decided it was “in” to be thin. The white female, American Type, definitely perceives her ideal body image much differently from her female counterpart even 20 years ago.
My book is about being thin too. But it is much more than that. It is about health and vitality as well as the vanity issue.
I tell my audiences that most women want to lose weight because of the vanity rather than health. And that’s okay.

It's nice to be your own thin self!

I lost 110 pounds nine years ago, and it is STILL OFF! And I did it by still eating the foods I was raised on - downhome style.
I think slim and I stay slim. I keep on growing this way through my program of action. Audiences ask me about the details too.
People often ask me about EXERCISE. Where does that fit in with my plan?
I have to tell you, when I lost my weight, I did not exercise. And that was a BIG MISTAKE. I tell audiences everywhere I should have exercised. I could have done something.
So, exercise. Of course, if you combine exercise, with proper foods, you can find an improved health conscious quality of life.

WITH MY BOOK....

What you will see is low-fat, homestyle cooking recipes at its best. People continually tell me how much they enjoyed my first book ***Natoma's Low Fat Homestyle Cooking***. And I'm grateful for that. Hardly a week goes by that someone does not let me know how pleased he/she is with the purchase of my first book. Just recently a strapping man who looked to be in his 40s or early 50s came by the LFC Centre office with his thirteen year old boy.

"I just wanted to stop and say thank you for your book," he said. He then went on to say how he bought the book and began cooking with the recipes since January of this year. He has lost some 54 pounds since then. And his son really enjoys the meals.

"I'm buying your book," someone else said to me, "because a friend of mine bought it, and she has lost weight with it."

Well if you liked my first book, you'll love this one. It's for you. Really. You can enjoy those comfort foods you were raised on. You can have your cake and eat it too.
This book's format is much the same as the first one. I've divided the recipes into the same groups. The style is much the same. Again, if you read and worked with the first book, you'll love this one too.

NUTRITIONAL ANALYSIS - HOW TO USE IT - VERY IMPORTANT

Nutritional analysis has been added to this book. Each recipe includes calculations of calories, protein, fat, carbohydrate, fiber, cholesterol and sodium. Over the past year many have asked me about such matters as **sodium and the role it plays** in my weight loss program.

My response to them is the same. If you have a problem with sodium, of course, you still have it with my program. For many, if not most, it is not an issue for them. But, again, see your personal physician about it before you go on any program.

We have deliberately tried to keep the sodium levels at an acceptable level for most items in this book. **With that in mind, you may want to salt and pepper your meals to your own liking.**

My encouragement for you is to avoid foods high in fats and be very careful about refined sugars if you're trying to lose weight.

A word about tomatoes. Some recipes call for fresh tomatoes in order to lower the SODIUM level. Again, if you do NOT have a sodium problem, you can use canned tomatoes to season the taste.

A word about serving portions in the analysis. Each recipe has a SERVING PORTION based upon a 1/2 cup portion. You may want to double the portion size for your own preference.

HOW THIS BOOK CAN HELP YOU

This is NOT a diet cookbook. There are plenty of them out there. My book is about a "thin for life" approach. You may be reading this book, and you're struggling with weight control for whatever reason. I want you to know that I could NOT have stayed on a diet for over eight years now. This is about a permanent way of life. It's a lifestyle. I consider myself a lifestyle coach.

I'm coaching you on how to make changes in your eating choices that gives you a feeling of more energy, better health, and a heightened sense of self-esteem.

DAILY LIVING CHALLENGES...

You'll read the sixty second Daily Living challenging uplifters in this book. They are designed to encourage you and get you thinking in ways you'll be strengthened.

These originally came from a fine couple in Louisville, Kentucky, Dick and Jo Lee who have a "Take 60" ministry. With their permission, I have adapted many of these sayings for you. At the end of this book you'll find a "Going Deeper" section. Here, you'll find Scripture references related to many of the essays in this book . It allows you to go deeper into spirituality if you desire.

Also after reading the text, with prayer you may want to get a piece of paper out and reflect back on the thoughts you read about and then circle which areas of your life that you feel this truth/s applies: Your financial life? Your spiritual life? Your social life? And so forth. At that point, you can consider different areas of your life such as financial, social, and religious for you to begin working on in terms of goals and so forth.

To dig deeper, you'll want to think about "my needs; my wants" and what you can do to apply this truth to each of your life areas.

It is a gradual process. You won't do it in 60 seconds.
You can make a start however.
Finally, fill in the sentence, " I will apply this to my ________life by ____.

____.

Intimacy. You can do it. Get to know yourself a little better.

Now, let's move on to the actual recipe section.

SECTION ONE

NEW PASSAGES - THERE'S ANOTHER LIFE FOR YOU

Recently, she did it again. Gail Sheehy has given us the fruit of her research about new life cycle changes (*New Passages).* You're in your 40s or 50s. Welcome to a new world!

AFTER 50

Women who reach 50 today - and remain free of cancer and heart disease - can expect to see their 92nd birthday. Hey, that's pretty good.
Are you a healthy 65-year old man? You can expect to live to 81, according to her. (*USA TODAY*, July 14, 1995, 7A).

LET'S GET STARTED ....

One of the things people tell me is how confused this whole business can be about healthy living - especially in the area of foods. Who can keep up with all of it?

So, what can you do?

For one thing, become better informed in the basics. Read on the following pages some basic information about how to "unravel" the mystery of food labels.

You can then go into the stores and be "forearmed" as you make choices about food.

That's what **Betty Harker,** Evansville, Indiana had to do. As a registered nurse she still struggled with weight-loss.
She came to the Low Fat Connection early last year because she tried a lot of other programs and it just didn't work for her. Even with a registered nurse background it didn't matter.

Today (August 1995) she has lost 67 pounds by using my recipes and learning how to work her plan to reach her own personal goals. She admits that it is so much different from the earlier programs.

Then, she would lose 10, 20, 25 pounds and then gain back 30. It was very hard on her self esteem as she went through the "yo-yo syndrome."

What about the rest of her family? Did Betty get a lot of support from them? Yes, her husband and other family members are strong in helping her. As she says, "Believe it or not we don't call this a diet at our house, we call it a change in lifestyle. I cook everything defatted and my husband has lost 12 pounds, my son is diabetic and he can eat it."

When Betty was about half way toward achieving her weight goals someone asked her about the rest of her weight goals. How concerned was she at the half-way mark. "I'm not worried about it," she said. " I take it one day at a time. You cannot lose it fast this way. I've been on the diet since March [1994, f.r.] so I'm averaging about six pounds a month. I have so much more energy, I feel like a different person."

And she is! She is now a certified registered nurse. She continues with her program. Her regular doctor encouraged her to go the low fat way. She is constantly letting people know what this kind of cooking can do for you.

Others have had great success with downhome low-fat cooking.

Consider Sue.

"My New Year's resolution for 1995, ('94,'93, and so and so on) was once again --- LOSE WEIGHT. But no matter how bad I wanted it, will power for me just doesn't exist. I tried the shakes, then I tried the pills. Then the pills gave me the shakes. It was just hopeless. I guess I had pretty much given up when I saw an ad in the paper about your grand opening. . . . I figured it was time for real help. I sure wasn't getting any smaller, not to mention any healthier.

After my first support meeting I was hooked. I could lose weight, drop inches eliminate the word DIET from my vocabulary, and still not be hungry and actually feel good. WOW What a concept, I love it. . . .

I'm not on a diet. I am on a lifestyle change. I am not a slave to my scales. . . .

With heart disease in my family history, I knew I had to make a change. I have definitely made the change. And it's change that I hope to live with, a whole lot longer than I would have if I would have kept up with my old ways of eating and living. . . .

I just want to thank you for helping me to get started on making all those changes and convincing me I CAN DO IT, for my life.

Keep up the good work."

Well, are you ready to begin to unravel some mysteries?: Let's get going.

UNRAVEL THE MYSTERY: FOOD LABELS

More Americans are learning about food labels. Until recently most of us had a hard time figuring out just what labels were to say to us. Then, the government stepped in and made various industries provide better accuracy on the labels.

Now, if you look at a label you'll find certain nutritional information. For example, take "Instant Quaker Oatmeal." The label lists nutrition information per serving for a daily diet of 2000 calories and a 2500 calories diet. 2500 calories is appropriate for many men or very physically active persons. Our example shows the following starting at the top of the listing:

First, you have nutrition facts with amount per serving.

Nutrition Facts
Serving Size - 1 packet (28g)
Servings Per Container 12

Amount Per Serving
Calories 100 Calories from Fat 20

	% of Daily Value*
Total Fat 2g	3%
Saturated Fat 0g	2%
Cholesterol 0mg	0%
Sodium 80mg	3%
Total Carbohydrate 19g	6%
Dietary Fiber 3g	10
Sugars 0g	
Protein 4 g	

In the space below you'll find usually vitamins and minerals information.

Vitamin A 25%

Then, you have % values based on a 2,000 or 2,500 requirement.
*Percents (%) of a Daily Value are based on a 2,000 Calorie diet. Your Daily Values may vary higher or lower depending on your calorie needs:

The new label laws effective May 1993 are designed to unravel the mystery of label reading. Consider the below material.

Serving Size = listed in household and metric measure

% Daily Value as listed on the label refers to a daily intake of 2000 calories established as the reference. This level was chosen because it has the greatest public health benefit for the nation. Check the preceding section on Dietary Guidelines for specific information.

Nutrients on label are declared as a percent of the Daily Value.

Example: Item with 40 milligrams of sodium would be 6% of the Daily Value of 2400 mg.
A food with 5 grams (gms) of saturated fat is 25% or 1/4 of the Total Daily Value of 20 g of saturated fat per 200 calories.

To further unravel the mystery, certain terms can be understood. Below are certain ***"Nutrient Content Descriptors"*** you can get familiar with for your low-fat journey.

Free - product contains no amount of or only trivial amounts of, one or more of these components: fat, saturated fat, cholesterol, sodium, sugars, and calories. For example, "calorie-free" means fewer than 5 calories per serving and "sugar free" and fat-free" both mean less than 0.5g per serving.

Low fat - 3 g or less per serving

Low saturated fat - 1 g or less per serving

Low sodium - less than 140 mg per serving

Very low sodium - less than 35 mg per serving

Low cholesterol - less than 20 mg per serving

Low calorie - 40 calories or less per serving

Lean and extra lean - These terms can be used to describe the fat content of meat, poultry, seafood and game meats.

Lean - less than 10 g fat, less than 4 g saturated fat, and less than 95 mg cholesterol per serving and per 100 g.

Extra lean - less than 5 g fat, less than 2 g saturated fat, and less than 95 mg cholesterol per serving and per 100 g.

High - This term can be used if the food contains 20 percent or more of the Daily Value for a particular nutrient.

***Good source* -** This term means that one serving of a food contains 10 to 19 percent of the Daily Value for a particular nutrient.

***Reduced* -** This term means that a nutritionally altered product contains 25 percent less of a nutrient or of calories than the regular or reference, product.

***Health claims* -** Claims for seven relationships between a nutrient or a food and the risk of a disease or health-related condition will be allowed for the first time.

***Calcium and osteoporosis* -** To carry this claim, a food must contain 120 percent or more of the Daily Value for calcium (200 mg) per serving, have a calcium content that equals or exceeds the food's content of phosphorus, and contain a form of calcium that can be readily absorbed and used by the body. The claim must name the target group most in need of adequate calcium intakes (that is, teens and young adult white and Asian women) and state the need for exercise and a healthy diet.

***Fat and cancer* -** To carry this claim, a food must meet the descriptor requirements for "low-fat" or, if fish and game meats, for "extra lean."

***Saturated fat and cholesterol and coronary heart disease (CHD)* -** This claim may be used if the food meets the definitions for the descriptors "low saturated fat," "low-cholesterol," and "low-fat."

Fiber - containing grain products, fruits and vegetables and cancer: To carry this claim , a food must be or must contain a grain product, fruit or vegetable and meet the descriptor requirements for "low-fat," and without fortification, be a "good source" of dietary fiber.

Fruits, vegetables and grains products that contain fiber and risk of CHD: To carry this claim, a food must be or must contain fruits, vegetables and grain products. It also must meet the descriptor requirements for "low saturated fat," "low-cholesterol," and "low-fat" and contain, without fortification, at least 0.6g soluble fiber per serving.

Sodium and hypertension (high blood pressure): To carry this claim, a food must meet the descriptor requirements for "low-sodium."

Fruits and vegetables and cancer: This claim may be made for fruits and vegetables that meet the descriptor requirements for "low-fat," and that, without fortification, for "good source" of at lease one of the following: dietary fiber or vitamins A or C.

Are you ready? Ready for some old-fashioned downhome cooking?
The next section starts the recipes. You'll be ready I'm sure to a start toward a better lifestyle.

One of the first things you can do is learn to make substitutions or find alternatives for high fat items.

The box on the next page shows you some options you can choose
from.

RECIPE ADJUSTMENT

Your favorite recipe can be adjusted to modify fat, sugar, or salt. Be creative and use your imagination.

Ingredients	***Suggested Substitutions***
1 whole egg	2 egg whites, 1/4 cup of egg substitute, whole grain flour is heavier than white flour, Fold in 3 egg whites to lighten the batter.
1 egg yolk	1 egg white
1 cup whole milk buttermilk	1 cup nonfat buttermilk, or 1 tablespoon lemon juice or vinegar added to 1 cup skim milk
Tomato products	Blend 1 can salt free tomato paste with 1 can of water to make puree, 2 cans of water to make sauce.
1 cup catsup	Mix 3/4 cup tomato paste, 2 tablespoons cider vinegar tablespoons water, garlic, tabasco sauce and lemon juice
White rice	Brown rice = 1/2 cup uncooked brown rice, cooked in 1 cup liquid 40-50 minutes equals 2 cups of cooked rice
1 cup all purpose white flour	1/2 cup whole wheat and 1/2 cup white flour or if recipe calls for several cups of flour, any of the following may replace 1 cup wheat flour: 3/4 cup rye flour, or 1 1/3 cup oatmeal
Sugar	Reduce the amount to 1/2 to 1/4 the original. 1 tablespoon fruit juice equals 1 teaspoon sugar. Replace 1 cup of sugar with 1 1/2 cups fruit juice concentrate and reduce liquid in recipe by 1/8 cup. Example: substitute applesauce for sugar in muffin or cake recipe.

Like A Child

What are children like?

They believe everything their fathers tell them, with no doubts.

They trust, and have faith in their fathers at all times.

They believe their fathers will provide for them. They know that their fathers love them. They know that their fathers can beat up anybody, any enemy.

They know that their fathers are always going to do what is best for them.

They know that they are safe in their fathers' arms.

They know their fathers' voice. They know that their fathers understand them.

You can add to this list, but in all that the child knows, he knows that he knows.

Our heavenly Father wants us to be like children with Him.

RECIPES FOR ALL SEASONS

BUSY DAY DRESSING CASSEROLE

1 box Stove Top stuffing (chicken flavor)
6 boneless skinless chicken breasts
1/2 can cream of celery soup
1/2 can cream of mushroom soup
2 small cans evaporated skim milk

METHOD:

Prepare stuffing mix as directed. Place 1/2 of the stuffing in a large baking dish. Heat the two soups and milk together. Place chicken on top of stuffing mix in baking dish. Add remaining stuffing mix over top of the chicken. Pour the soup mixture over all. Bake at 350 degrees for 40 minutes.

SERVES: 6

FAT GRAMS PER SERVING: 8

Nutritional Analysis Per Serving:

cal	*g. fat*	*(% of cal)*	*g.fib*	*mg. chol*	*mg. sod*
271	*8*	*26*	*0.46*	*23*	*1346*

CORNBREAD FAT FREE

2 cups SELF-RISING yellow cornmeal
1/4 cup applesauce sweetened
1 egg white
1 cup skim milk

METHOD:

Mix the above ingredients until well-moistened.
Spray 9-inch pan or muffin tin with non-stick cooking spray.
Bake in 425-degree oven about 15 minutes for muffin and 15-20 minutes for cake pan.

SERVES: 8

FATS PER SERVING: FAT FREE

Nutritional Analysis Per Serving:

cal	*g. fat*	*(%of cal)*	*g.fib*	*mg.chol*	*mg. sod*
49	*0.21*	*4*	*.11*	*.50*	*137*

ROAST TURKEY

Preheat oven to 350 degrees.
1 8-pound young turkey
2 tablespoons lemon juice
1 teaspoon salt
1/4 teaspoon each of thyme and rosemary
1 cup raw celery
1 peeled onion
6 sprigs of parsley
3/4 cup FAT FREE chicken broth

METHOD:

Wash and pat dry turkey, inside and out, with paper towels. Discard any excess fat.
Sprinkle cavity of the bird with lemon juice and rub remaining juice into the skin.
Sprinkle the bird's cavity with the herbs and salt and fill with the vegetables.
Truss the bird and rub 1/2 teaspoon salt into the skin.
Bake on a rack in a sprayed shallow roaster covered with a loose foil tent.
Bake 2 hours.
Remove foil tent and baste with FAT FREE broth.
Continue baking 30 minutes more or until leg moves freely (180 degrees if using a meat thermometer.)
Let sit 5 or more minutes, open cavity and discard vegetables.
Carve, discarding skin.

SERVES: 15

FAT GRAMS PER SERVING: 8

Nutritional Analysis Per Serving:

cal	*g. fat*	*(% of cal)*	*g.fib*	*mg. chol*	*mg. sod*
161	*8*	*42*	*0.36*	*75*	*133*

How Do You Cast Your Cares?

Peter was a fisherman and he knew what it meant to cast his net on the qater. Being a fisherman, he knew where to toss the net (most of the time) to catch the fish.

The fish were the answer to his problems, his job, his income, his food and his welfare.

When we cast our net and the problems don't seem to go away, or answers aren't caught in or net, what then?

Peter had been fishing like other times, but without any success, when Jesus told him where to cast his net. Because He cares for us and He knows where all the fish are, why not ask him.

We have not because we ask not.

The way to ask or cast your care on Him is through prayer.

CRANBERRY PINEAPPLE TREAT

5/8 ounce package SUGAR FREE cherry Jello mix
2 cups boiling water
1 16-ounce can whole cranberry sauce
2 cups drained, crushed pineapple, in its own juice, reserving juice.
11/2 cups reserved juice, adding water if necessary.

METHOD:

Dissolve Jello in boiling water.
Mix in the whole cranberry sauce, blending well.
Add the pineapple juice and mix well.
Chill until slightly thickened and add pineapple.
Chill until firm.

SERVES: 12

FAT GRAMS PER SERVING: FAT FREE

Nutritional Analysis Per Serving:

cal	*g. fat*	*(% of cal)*	*g.fib*	*mg. chol*	*mg. sod*
88	*.06*	*.1*	*.81*	*0.00*	*64*

SAVORY MASHED POTATOES

6 medium potatoes, peeled
1 8-ounce package FAT FREE cream cheese
1 cup FAT FREE sour cream
1 tablespoon chopped chives
2 teaspoons salt
1/4 teaspoon pepper
1 clove garlic, crushed OR 1/2 teaspoon garlic powder
1/4 teaspoon paprika

METHOD:

Cook potatoes in boiling salted water until tender.
Drain.
In a large bowl, mash potatoes with an electric mixer.
Add cream cheese and sour cream, pepper and garlic.
Beat on high speed until smooth and light.
Stir in chives.
Spoon into a baking dish that has been sprayed with butter-flavored cooking spray.
Sprinkle with paprika.
Bake 30 minutes in a 350-degree oven or until golden brown and heated through.
This can also be prepared ahead of time and frozen before baking.

SERVES: 8

FAT GRAMS PER SERVING: FAT FREE

Nutritional Analysis Per Serving:

cal	*g. fat*	*(%of cal)*	*g.fib*	*mg.chol*	*mg. sod*
422	*.46*	*1*	*7.34*	*8*	*381*

SAGE DRESSING

1 loaf FAT FREE bread, dried overnight and torn into bite-size pieces (or 9 inch pan of fat free cornbread, not in below analysis)
3 cups FAT FREE chicken broth, either homemade and defatted OR ready to use CANNED
1 cup diced celery
1 cup diced onion
1 teaspoon (or more) dried sage
1/2 teaspoon pepper
5/8 teaspoon dried basil
1/4 cup fat free egg substitute

METHOD:

Cook onion and celery in 1 1/2 cups water until tender.
In a large mixing bowl, combine vegetables and remaining liquid, bread and seasonings.
Slowly add chicken broth, using enough to thoroughly moisten bread.
Stir in fat free egg substitute and, if needed, more broth.
Pour into a baking dish that has been sprayed with butter-flavored cooking spray.
Smooth evenly in dish and spray top with butter-flavored cooking spray.
Bake 30-40 minutes in a 350-degree oven until nicely brown on top.

SERVES: 8

FAT GRAMS PER SERVING: FAT FREE

Nutritional Analysis Per Serving:

cal	g. fat	(% of cal)	g.fib	mg. chol	mg. sod
190	0.05	1	6	0.00	431

SOUPER GREEN BEANS

2 cans French-style green beans
2 teaspoons dry onion soup mix with mushrooms

METHOD:

Drain liquid from one can of the green beans.
Place beans and 2nd can of beans in sauce pan.
Stir in dry soup mix.
Stir well to mix and bring to a boil.
Reduce heat, cover and simmer for 45 minutes to an hour

SERVES: 8

FAT GRAMS PER SERVING: FAT FREE

Nutritional Analysis Per Serving:

cal	*g. fat*	*(%of cal)*	*g.fib*	*mg.chol*	*mg. sod*
18	*0.15*	*7*	*0.00*	*0.00*	*352*

SENSATIONAL DOUBLE LAYER PUMPKIN PIE

1 cup FAT FREE cream cheese
1 tablespoon skim milk
1 tablespoon sugar
11/2 cups thawed LITE whipped topping
1 graham cracker pie crust
(SEE RECIPE for crust on page 40)
1 cup skim milk
3 ounces SUGAR FREE vanilla instant pudding
1 16-ounce can of pumpkin
1 teaspoon ground cinnamon
1/2 teaspoon ground ginger
1/4 teaspoon ground cloves

METHOD:

Soften cream cheese and mix with a tablespoon of milk and sugar in a large bowl. Using a wire whisk, beat until smooth. Gently stir in lite whipped topping and spread mixture on bottom of crust.
Pour 1 cup milk into a bowl and add pudding mix.
Whisk until well blended, 1-2 minutes. (Mixture will be thick)
Stir in pumpkin and the spices using the whisk.
Spread over the cream cheese mixture.
Refrigerate at least 3 hours.
Garnish with more lite whipped topping if desired.

SERVES: 8

FAT GRAMS PER SERVING: 3

Nutritional Analysis Per Serving:

cal	*g. fat*	*(% of cal)*	*g.fib*	*mg. chol*	*mg. sod*
254	*3*	*9*	*3.26*	*5*	*848*

Looking For Something To Do??

How about visiting the orphans and widows in their distress?

Feed the hungry. Give water to the thirsty. Care for those in prison perhaps?

Look around and be opened to opportunities.

Call someone -- reach out!

Send someone a card or letter --

Stop by to just say hello or bake a cake.

Help someone in their time of need.

Looking for something to do?

FRUIT DESSERT

1 can pineapple in juice
1 large can peaches drained (cut in small pieces)
10 ounce strawberries in juice frozen, unsweetened
4 bananas
1 small package instant SUGAR FREE vanilla pudding (dry)
2 tablespoons famous orange drink mix (I prefer Tang)

METHOD:

Mix all together in a large bowl.

SERVES: 12

FAT GRAMS PER SERVING: FAT FREE

Nutritional Analysis Per Serving:

cal	*g. fat*	*(% of cal)*	*g.fib*	*mg. chol*	*mg. sod*
114	*0.32*	*3*	*2.21*	*0.00*	*114*

NIGHT BEFORE CASSEROLE

1/2 pound thin sliced package of 94% FAT FREE ham
12 slices FAT FREE bread
6 slices FAT FREE American cheese
Prepared mustard
1 carton fat free egg substitute (equals 4 eggs)
3 cups skim milk
1/2 can cream of mushroom soup, undiluted
Dash Worcestershire sauce
Dash tabasco sauce
1/3 cup skim milk

METHOD:

Spread mustard on 6 slices of the bread, after removing crusts. Place in the bottom of a 9 x 13 baking dish that has been sprayed with butter-flavored cooking spray. Top each piece of bread with a slice of the FAT FREE cheese, then a layer of the thin sliced ham.
Spread mustard on other 6 slices of bread, after removing crusts, and place on the ham slices.
Mix with an electric mixer the 3 cups of milk and the carton of egg substitute.
Pour over all and cover with foil. Refrigerate overnight.
Bake the next day at 300 degrees for 1 hour.
Let stand 5 minutes before serving.
Meanwhile, mix 1/2 can of soup with the 1/3 cup milk and tabasco and Worcestershire sauces and heat to boiling.
Serve over casserole. Great for Sunday breakfast.

SERVES: 8

FAT GRAMS PER SERVING: 3

Nutritional Analysis Per Serving:

cal	*g. fat*	*(%of cal)*	*g.fib*	*mg.chol*	*mg. sod*
254	*2.94*	*10*	*3.06*	*22*	*1137*

APPLE PANCAKES

1 cup flour
1/2 teaspoon salt
2 teaspoons sugar
1/4 cup fat free egg substitute
1 cup skim milk
2 teaspoons vegetable oil
5 medium-size apples, peeled and thinly sliced

METHOD:

Combine milk, fat free egg substitutes and oil.
Add to dry ingredients that have been blended in a small bowl.
Fold in apples.
Pour batter into a sprayed Teflon skillet and
spread to a 5-inch circle.
Turn when bubbles form and cook second side until
golden brown and apples are tender.

MAKES 4 PANCAKES.

FAT GRAMS PER SERVING: 3 PER PANCAKE

Nutritional Analysis Per Serving:

cal	*g. fat*	*(% of cal)*	*g.fib*	*mg. chol*	*mg. sod*
253	*3*	*11*	*4.21*	*1*	*149*

Did You Ever Plant a Shade Tree?

Have you ever planted a shade tree by a house or patio knowing that it would take years before you would realize the full benefit of the tree? Sometimes we move before we ever get to enjoy any of the shade.

The Good Book is like that sometimes. It may take years before we see any results or we may not even be there when it produces the shade.

When we look at a beautiful tree, we forget that it took years for the tree to reach its full maturity.

When we see a spiritually mature person and want to be like him, we must not forget the time it took him to mature. We must also remember that it takes time for some of the new Christians we see to grow into maturity.

WING DING MUFFINS

Preheat oven to 375 degrees.
1 can low-fat biscuits
1 pound lean ground round
1/2 cup catsup
3 tablespoons brown sugar substitute
1 tablespoon vinegar
1 teaspoon chili powder
1 cup shredded FAT FREE Cheddar cheese

METHOD:

Spray muffin tin with non-stick cooking spray. Set aside.
Separate biscuits and pat out
on flat surface into 5-inch rounds.
Press in the bottom and up the sides of muffin cup.
Set aside.
Brown the meat, drain well on paper towels
and return to skillet.
In a small bowl, mix catsup, brown sugar, vinegar and chili powder, stirring until smooth.
Add to the meat and mix well.
Divide the mixture among the biscuit-lined
muffin cups, then sprinkle each with cheese.
Bake 18-20 minutes or until golden brown.
Cool about 5 minutes before removing from the tin.
Serve with a hearty green salad.

SERVES: 10

FAT GRAMS PER SERVING: 3

Nutritional Analysis Per Serving:

cal	*g. fat*	*(% of cal)*	*g.fib*	*mg. chol*	*mg. sod*
170	*3.07*	*16*	*.55*	*28*	*707*

RIBBON DESSERT

1 cup sugar OR 4 packs sweetener (DO NOT USE EQUAL)
2 cups skim milk
2 packages unflavored gelatin
2 cups FAT FREE sour cream
2 teaspoons vanilla
1 .3 ounce package each of SUGAR FREE lime, lemon, orange and cherry Jello

METHOD:

Spray a 9 x 13 glass dish with non-stick cooking spray.
Bring skim milk to a boil and add sugar OR sweetener.
Remove from heat and add gelatin that has been dissolved in a small amount of water to the milk.
Place in a blender and add the sour cream and vanilla.
Blend for 2 minutes, scraping down sides.
Prepare the flavored Jello, one box at a time, using 1 cup of boiling water and 1/2 cup cold water.
Pour into the bottom of the glass dish, chill until set.
When firm, pour 1 1/2 cups of the sour cream mixture on top and again chill until set.
Continue until all the flavors and sour cream mixture have been layered.
Chill and cut into squares.
Serve with a dollop of lite whipped topping for a beautiful lo-cal dessert.

SERVES: 8

FAT GRAMS PER SERVING: FAT FREE

Nutritional Analysis Per Serving:

cal	*g. fat*	*(%of cal)*	*g.fib*	*mg.chol*	*mg. sod*
151	*0.10*	*1*	*0.00*	*9*	*218*

LOW FAT GRAHAM CRACKER CRUST

8 inch crust:
1 1/4 crumbs (about 18 low fat graham crackers)
2 tablespoons sugar
1/4 cup melted fat free margarine

METHOD:

Heat oven to 350 degrees.
Mix crumbs, sugar and margarine.
Reserve 3 tablespoons of mixture for topping if desired.
Press remaining mixture firmly against bottom and side of pie plate.
Bake at 350 degrees for 10 minutes.
Cool.

SERVES: 6

FAT GRAMS PER SERVING: 3

Nutritional Analysis Per Serving:

cal	g. fat	(% of cal)	g.fib	mg. chol	mg. sod
291	3.00	9	2.00	0.00	780

"PLUM DELICIOUS" BAKED HAM

1 3-to-5 pound 95% FAT FREE, fully cooked boneless ham
2 jars plum baby food dessert (junior size) for glaze

METHOD:

Line 9 x 13 baking dish with heavy-duty foil.
Place rack in pan and put ham on it.
Bake slow in a 200-degree oven
for about 4 hours to heat through.
Cover ham with the plum "glaze" and bake 1/2 hour more,
adding "glaze" as a baste.

SERVES: 10

FAT GRAMS PER SERVING: 6

Nutritional Analysis Per Serving:

cal	g. fat	(%of cal)	g.fib	mg.chol	mg. sod
194	5.60	26	0.40	98	1458

SWEET POTATO CASSEROLE

3 cups mashed sweet potatoes
1/2 cup sugar
1/2 cup fat free egg substitute
1 teaspoon vanilla
4 tablespoons famous brand FAT FREE margarine

METHOD:

Mix together, put into sprayed casserole dish.
Top with:
Brown sugar substitute - should equal 1 cup of brown sugar
1/3 cup flour
1/3 cup FAT FREE famous brand margarine
1 cup substitute brown sugar
3/8 cup white flour
3/8 cup fat free margarine

METHOD:

Rub above ingredients together and sprinkle over sweet potatoes.
Bake at 350 degrees for 30 minutes.

SERVES: 6

FAT GRAMS PER SERVING: FAT FREE

WATCH THOSE CALORIES!

Nutritional Analysis Per Serving:

cal	*g. fat*	*(% of cal)*	*g.fib*	*mg. chol*	*mg. sod*
199	*0.32*	*1*	*0.18*	*0.00*	*262*

Give Thanks

It's that time of year when we think about giving thanks.

So many of us get caught up in keeping up with the Jones that we aren't thankful because there are still so many things we don't have. The man who had no shoes complained until he saw the man with no feet.

It's time to look at the less fortunate and be thankful for what we have.

Not only our food and clothing, but for the friends that we have --

the people that gave us an encouraging word today -- that prepared your meals -- gave you a smile -- called you on the phone -- held the door open for you -- for the blue in the sky -- the leaves on the trees, and the colors and shade they provide -- for the love of a Peter -- the writer or singer of a song that lifts our spirits -- for a country where we are free to worship.

CORN SOUFFLE

2 cups cream-style corn (NOTE: Make sure nutritional label reads TOTAL FAT 0)
2 tablespoons flour
1 carton fat free egg substitute (equals 4 eggs)
2 cups skim milk
4 slices FAT FREE bread
1 tablespoon FAT FREE famous brand margarine (melted)
4 slices FAT FREE bread made into crumbs

METHOD:

Combine first 5 ingredients
and mix lightly.
Put in a casserole dish that has been sprayed with
butter-flavored cooking spray.
Top with the bread crumbs.
Drizzle crumbs with melted margarine.
Bake for 30 minutes at 350 degrees or until bubbly.

SERVES: 4

FAT GRAMS PER SERVING: FAT FREE

Nutritional Analysis Per Serving:

cal	*g. fat*	*(% of cal)*	*g.fib*	*mg. chol*	*mg. sod*
359	*0.24*	*0.00*	*5.10*	*2*	*959*

SUNSET SALAD

0.6 ounce package SUGAR FREE orange Jello
1/2 teaspoon salt
1 2/3 cups boiling water
1 cup chunk pineapple in juice
1 tablespoon lemon juice OR vinegar
1 cup grated carrots

METHOD:

Dissolve Jello and salt in boiling water.
Add pineapple and juice
Add carrots and lemon juice (or vinegar).
Chill 2 hours.

SERVES: 6

FAT GRAMS PER SERVING: FAT FREE

Nutritional Analysis Per Serving:

cal	*g. fat*	*(%of cal)*	*g.fib*	*mg.chol*	*mg. sod*
246	*0.34*	*1*	*3.16*	*0.00*	*168*

RED VELVET LIGHT CAKE

1/2 cup FAT FREE, low-calorie margarine
4 ounces FAT FREE cream cheese
1 1/2 cups sugar
1/2 cup fat free egg substitute
2 1-ounce bottles red food coloring
2 1/4 cups sifted cake flour
2 tablespoons unsweetened cocoa
1 teaspoon baking soda
1/4 teaspoon salt
1 cup LOW FAT buttermilk
1 teaspoon vanilla

METHOD:

Beat margarine and cream cheese at medium speed with mixer until creamy.
Gradually add the sugar, beating well after each addition.
Stir egg substitute in food coloring
Gradually add egg substitute, beating after each addition.
Combine flour and next 3 ingredients; add to margarine mixture alternately with buttermilk, beginning and ending with flour.
Mix just until blended.
Pour batter into three 9-inch cake pans coated with cooking spray.
Bake at 350 degrees for 18 minutes or until done.
Cool in pans on wire rack.
Remove from pans and cool completely on racks.
Spread frosting (see page 154 for frosting directions) between layers and over top and sides of cake.
SERVES: 16

FAT GRAMS PER SERVING: FAT FREE

Nutritional Analysis Per Serving:

cal	*g. fat*	*(% of cal)*	*g.fib*	*mg. chol*	*mg. sod*
99	*0.45*	*4*	*0.46*	*2*	*191*

*Nutritional Analysis does not include frosting.

Hurt Feelings?

Has someone hurt your feelings recently?

The Good Book says pray for those who mistreat you. That isn't the world's way.

A joyful heart is a good medicine, but a broken spirit dries up the bones.

God knows that if you keep that hurt inside of you, it can cause sickness "forgive." Forgive as He forgives those who trespass against Him.

He has removed our transgressions as far as the east is from the west.

We need to learn this spiritual principle and forgive.

God only tells us to do what is best for us and others.

Learn to release -- the pain and hurt inside -- a healthy release is healthy for your soul.

APPETIZERS

INDEX FOR APPETIZERS

25 Hour Day?

Do you need a 25-hour day?

Maybe you need a 30-hour day?

Sometimes we wish that today would get over quick.

We may want God to do something dramatic for us --that may not happen-- but He can cause things to fall into place so it seems that you are able to get a whole lot more done in a short period of time.

How can this happen?

Do not neglect spiritual principles and concepts. Keep them in your heart. Add to your quality of life. Peace will be added to you.

CORNED BEEF DIP

1 8-ounce can corned beef
2 packages (8 ounce) Fat free cream cheese
6 ounce bottle horseradish

METHOD:

Mix in blender or mixer on high speed.

SERVES: 6

FAT GRAMS PER SERVING: 6

Nutritional Analysis Per Serving:

cal	g. fat	(%of cal)	g.fib	mg.chol	mg. sod
160	5.7	32	0.26	41	699

CREAMY CUCUMBER ONION DIP

1 pouch onion soup (dry) mix
1 8-ounce package fat free cream cheese, softened
1 cup fat free plain yogurt
1 medium cucumber, peeled, seeded and shredded
1/4 cup chopped pimento
1/4 cup chopped green onion

METHOD:

Blend soup mix, cream cheese and yogurt.
Stir in cucumbers, pimento and green onion.
Cover and chill 2 hours.
Serve with chips or cut up raw vegetables.

SERVES: 4

FAT GRAMS PER SERVING: FAT FREE

Nutritional Analysis Per Serving:

cal	*g. fat*	*(% of cal)*	*g.fib*	*mg. chol*	*mg. sod*
136	*0.05*	*0.33*	*0.37*	*9*	*1649*

DIP FOR VEGETABLES

8 ounces fat free sour cream
16 ounces fat free mayonnaise
1 teaspoon celery salt
1 tablespoon garlic powder
1 teaspoon onion powder

METHOD:

Mix all together and put in a tight container. Refrigerate.

SERVES: 6

FAT GRAMS PER SERVING: FAT FREE

Nutritional Analysis Per Serving:

cal	g. fat	(%of cal)	g.fib	mg.chol	mg. sod
71	0.00	0.00	0.02	2	861

DIP-N-FRUIT

7 ounces marshmallow cream
3 ounces fat free cream cheese

METHOD:

Mix the above together.

SERVES: 5 (2 OUNCE PORTIONS)

FAT GRAMS PER SERVING: FAT FREE

Nutritional Analysis Per Serving:

cal	g. fat	(% of cal)	g.fib	mg. chol	mg. sod
148	0.00	0.00	0.00	2	144

Fear?

Many of us don't get involved with what God has called us to because of fear.

Fear of failure, fear of people, fear of speaking, fear of rejection and the list goes on.

Don't let fear stop you.

Trust Him to give you the strength to help you.

FRUIT DIP

8 ounce fat free sour cream
1.34 ounce box sugar free instant vanilla pudding
1 cup skim milk (more or less or as needed to make it thick as you would like)

METHOD:

Mix well and refrigerate.

SERVES: 4

FAT GRAMS PER SERVING: FAT FREE

Nutritional Analysis Per Serving:

cal	*g. fat*	*(% of cal)*	*g.fib*	*mg. chol*	*mg. sod*
140	*0.10*	*0.00*	*0.00*	*5*	*1209*

Love Is Still Working

The Good Book says there is no fear in love, but perfect love casts out all fear.

That means if you are walking in God's love you won't steal, kill, covet, have other gods (whatever you love more than God), commit adultery and so on.

God's love is what we need to be so full of, that we can then overcome all sin.

Faith, hope and love, these three; the greatest of these is love.

MUSHROOM SPREAD

8 ounce package fat free sour cream
1 small can mushrooms, chopped fine
1 cup grated onion or to taste
1 teaspoon drop Tabasco sauce
1/4 teaspoon garlic salt or to taste

METHOD:

Mix together with fat free mayonnaise to right consistency.

SERVES: 4

FAT GRAMS PER SERVING: FAT FREE

Nutritional Analysis Per Serving:

cal	*g. fat*	*(% of cal)*	*g.fib*	*mg. chol*	*mg. sod*
48	*0.07*	*1*	*0.83*	*4*	*99*

NOTES

NACHOS

1 pound lean ground sirloin
1 large onion, chopped
1 teaspoon seasoned salt
1/2 teaspoon ground cumin
2 cans (1 pound each) fat free refried beans
1 package (1 1/4 ounce) taco seasoning mix
2 cups shredded fat free sharp shredded cheese
1 can (4 ounce) chopped green chilies, drained
1 cup shredded fat free Cheddar cheese
3/4 cup chunky taco sauce
28 baked tortilla chips
1/2 cup fat free sour cream
1/2 cup chopped green onions

NACHOS CONT'D

METHOD:

Brown meat and onion; pat dry.
Add seasoned salt and cumin.
Combine beans, taco seasoning mix and sharp shredded cheese; mix well.
Spread beans in a shallow, oval 15x10-inch baking dish; cover with meat mixture.
Sprinkle chilies over meat; top with Cheddar cheese.
Pour taco sauce over cheese.
Bake, uncovered in preheated 400 degree oven 20 to 25 minutes, or until thoroughly heated.
Tuck tortilla chips around edge of platter; garnish as desired with 1/2 cup sour cream and 1/2 cup green onions.

SERVES: 10

FAT GRAMS PER SERVING: 2

Nutritional Analysis Per Serving:

cal	*g. fat*	*(%of cal)*	*g.fib*	*mg.chol*	*mg. sod*
291	*2.40*	*7*	*5.05*	*33*	*1794*

PARTY-TIME SPINACH DIP

1 envelope vegetable soup mix with beef stock
1 pint fat free sour cream
1/4 teaspoon garlic powder
1 10-ounce package frozen chopped spinach, thawed and well drained

METHOD:

In medium bowl, combine all ingredients; chill. Serve with Fat free crackers or fresh vegetables.

SERVES: 6

FAT GRAMS PER SERVING: 1

Nutritional Analysis Per Serving:

cal	*g. fat*	*(% of cal)*	*g.fib*	*mg. chol*	*mg. sod*
141	*0.90*	*6*	*1.62*	*12*	*779*

SALMON DIP

1 large can pink salmon
1 8-ounce package fat free cream cheese
2 tablespoons grated onion
1 tablespoon lemon juice
1 tablespoon horseradish

METHOD:

Mix together and refrigerate for 2 hours, then form into a ball. Roll in parsley flakes.

SERVES: 7

FAT GRAMS PER SERVING: 2

Nutritional Analysis Per Serving:

cal	*g. fat*	*(%of cal)*	*g.fib*	*mg.chol*	*mg. sod*
100	*2.07*	*19*	*0.07*	*36*	*196*

SHRIMP SPREAD

1 large onion
1/2 bell pepper
1/2 pint fat free mayonnaise
2 tablespoons sweet relish
1 cup crushed Fat free cracker crumbs
2 sticks celery
2 pounds shrimp, peeled

METHOD:

Season to taste.
Mince onion and bell pepper; chop celery.
Boil shrimp lightly, then chop them and combine all the ingredients with mayonnaise and sweet relish.
Add cracker crumbs and season to taste.

SERVES: 4

FAT GRAMS PER SERVING: 3

Nutritional Analysis Per Serving:

cal	*g. fat*	*(% of cal)*	*g.fib*	*mg. chol*	*mg. sod*
397	*2.64*	*6*	*2.15*	*443*	*1047*

SHRIMP DIP

1/2 cup skim milk
1 pound boiled, chopped shrimp
2 teaspoons lemon juice
1 teaspoon garlic powder
2 8-ounce packages fat free cream cheese, softened
2 teaspoons Worcestershire sauce

METHOD:

Blend milk and cheese until creamy. Stir in shrimp, Add lemon juice, garlic powder, worcestershire.
Mix well.
Stir in shrimp.

SERVES: 6

FAT GRAMS PER SERVING: 1

Nutritional Analysis Per Serving:

cal	*g. fat*	*(%of cal)*	*g.fib*	*mg.chol*	*mg. sod*
149	*0.86*	*5*	*0.01*	*158*	*558*

Holiday Season

This may be the time of year when families and friends get together.

The holiday season. It is also the time of year when there are more suicides.

Why? Because many people are very lonely - they are from broken homes - maybe the loss of a loved one - out of work - no place to stay - or no money.

It is that time of year when all the holiday glitter, and people walking arm in arm, makes them feel even more lonely.

Do your part to help this year.

Share some love with someone.

A smile, a few minutes of your time, invite someone home, share a ride, send a card, pay a visit, buy a lunch, send some flowers, show that you care, and give them a hug.

You may be helping someone more than you know.

SHRIMP DIP OR SPREAD

2 pounds boiled shrimp, chopped coarsely
16 ounce package fat free cream cheese
16 ounce fat free sour cream
1 package dry Italian fat free dressing mix
6 tablespoons Worcestershire sauce
1/4 teaspoon tabasco

METHOD:

Mix all ingredients (except shrimp) thoroughly.
Stir in chopped shrimp.
Serve with wheat crackers.

SERVES: 6

FAT GRAMS PER SERVING: 2

Nutritional Analysis Per Serving:

cal	*g. fat*	*(%of cal)*	*g.fib*	*mg.chol*	*mg. sod*
269	*1.63*	*5*	*0.00*	*310*	*1594*

SOFT TACOS CON PASAS

1 pound lean ground sirloin
1 (1 1/4 ounce) package taco seasoning mix
1/2 cup water
1 (8-ounce) can tomato sauce
1/2 cup raisins
8 fat free tortillas
2 1/2 tablespoons Fat free melted margarine
1 cup shredded fat free Cheddar cheese

METHOD:

Brown sirloin until crumbly; drain fat.
Add taco seasoning mix, water, tomato sauce and raisins; bring to a boil.
Reduce heat and simmer, uncovered, 20 minutes.
Brush tortillas with melted margarine, brown lightly in a non-stick skillet.
Spoon taco meat filling on tortillas; sprinkle with cheddar cheese.
Fold to enclose.

SERVES: 8

FAT GRAMS PER SERVING: 3

Nutritional Analysis Per Serving:

cal	*g. fat*	*(% of cal)*	*g.fib*	*mg. chol*	*mg. sod*
272	*2.93*	*10*	*2.16*	*35*	*1272*

SPINACH DIP

1 cup fat free mayonnaise
1 cup fat free sour cream
8 ounces fat free cream cheese
1 package frozen, chopped spinach
1 tablespoon minced onion
1 package fat free dressing
1 tablespoon chives

METHOD:

Cook and drain spinach well.
Mix together all remaining ingredients with spinach.
Serve with carrots, celery, cauliflower, etc.

SERVES: 12

FAT GRAMS PER SERVING: FAT FREE

Nutritional Analysis Per Serving:

cal	*g. fat*	*(%of cal)*	*g.fib*	*mg.chol*	*mg. sod*
65	*0.08*	*1*	*0.74*	*5*	*641*

CASSEROLES

INDEX TO CASSEROLES

BEAN-SAUSAGE CASSEROLE

3 1-pound cans kidney beans, drained
6 strips turkey bacon, diced
1 pound Mr. Turkey polish sausage, cut in 8 strips
1 cup chopped onion
1/4 teaspoon pepper
1/2 cup water

METHOD:

Fry bacon bits until crisp; discard fat.
Combine all ingredients in slow cooker.
Cook on low 8-10 hours, on high 5 hours, or on automatic 6 hours.

SERVES: 8

FAT GRAMS PER SERVING: 5

Nutritional Analysis Per Serving:

cal	*g. fat*	*(% of cal)*	*g.fib*	*mg. chol*	*mg. sod*
378	*4.46*	*11*	*0.33*	*33*	*1913*

Age

is a very interesting subject.

When you are small, you aren't five or six, but five and a half. Then you are almost sixteen. How about in two months, I will be twenty-one. Things change for many at age thirty.

To many, thirty was a threshold into a group that you never wanted to be a part of. Many people joke about staying thirty-nine. At fifty, a half-century, and downhill from here on.

A few more years and the talk changes again. In two years I will retire (almost sixty-five). Then it sounds like the kids again. Going on seventy-five.

Next year, I will be ninety. Do you know that in three years, I will be a hundred? Age really is funny. Our age as a Christian is funny too.

How we talk about our age as a Christian sometimes is influenced by what we think we have done for the Lord. Before you let that put any condemnation on you and you start to compare yourself to others like the world does, remember that there is no condemnation in Christ Jesus. He just loves us. What are a few years in eternity anyway?

BROCCOLI-SPINACH CASSEROLE

2 10-ounce each packages frozen broccoli cuts
1 10-ounce package frozen chopped spinach
1/4 cup minced onion
4 ounces fat free egg substitute
1 10 3/4-ounce can cream of mushroom soup
3/4 cup fat free mayonnaise
1/4 teaspoon pepper
1 cup shredded fat free Cheddar cheese
1 cup herb-seasoned stuffing cubes

METHOD:

Combine broccoli, spinach and onion in 3-quart casserole dish.
Cook, covered, on full power for 14 to 17 minutes, or until done. Stir halfway through cooking time to break apart.
Drain very well.
Beat egg substitute in 2-quart casserole dish.
Stir in soup, mayonnaise, and pepper.
Add vegetables.
Heat, covered, on full power for 6 to 8 minutes, or until heated through.
Stir halfway through heating time.
Combine cheese and stuffing mix and sprinkle on casserole during last minute of heating time.

SERVES: 12

FAT GRAMS PER SERVING: 3

Nutritional Analysis Per Serving:

cal	*g. fat*	*(% of cal)*	*g.fib*	*mg. chol*	*mg. sod*
168	*2.81*	*15*	*1.57*	*2*	*793*

BUSY DAY DRESSING CASSEROLE

1 box Stove Top stuffing (chicken flavor)
6 boneless skinless chicken breasts
1/2 can cream of celery soup
1/2 can cream of mushroom soup
2 small cans evaporated skim milk
2 tablespoon fat free margarine

METHOD:

Prepare stuffing mix as directed.
Place 1/2 of the stuffing in a large baking dish.
Heat the two soups and milk together.
Place chicken on top of stuffing mix in baking dish.
Add remaining stuffing mix over top of the chicken.
Pour the soup mixture over all.
Bake at 350 degrees for 40 minutes or until done.

SERVES: 6

FAT GRAMS PER SERVING: 8

Nutritional Analysis Per Serving:

cal	*g. fat*	*(%of cal)*	*g.fib*	*mg.chol*	*mg. sod*
271	*7.68*	*26*	*0.46*	*23*	*1346*

CABBAGE DISH CASSEROLE

1 small cabbage (cut in half)
1 pound lean ground sirloin
1 green pepper (chopped)
1 onion (chopped)
1 10 1/2-ounce can tomato soup

METHOD:

Spread half of the cabbage in a baking dish.
Fry meat with the green pepper and onion.
Drain meat mixture.
Put half of the mixture over the cabbage.
Add rest of cabbage and top with meat.
Spread tomato soup over top and bake at 350 degrees for 45 minutes.

SERVES: 6

FAT GRAMS PER SERVING: 4

Nutritional Analysis Per Serving:

cal	*g. fat*	*(% of cal)*	*g.fib*	*mg. chol*	*mg. sod*
146	*3.57*	*22*	*2.43*	*35*	*398*

CARROT CASSEROLE

2 cups carrots
1 cup fat free sharp cheese, grated
8 ounces fat free egg substitute
1 cup fat free bread crumbs
1 1/4 cup skim milk
1/4 teaspoon pepper
1/4 teaspoon cayenne pepper

METHOD:

Grate 10 carrots.
Cover with water and cook 15 minutes.
Drain.
This makes 2 cups carrots.
Then add cheese, eggs, milk, pepper and cayenne pepper to taste and top with bread crumbs.
Place in sprayed and floured casserole dish.
Bake in casserole placed in pan of water at 325 degrees for 1 hour.

SERVES: 4

FAT GRAMS PER SERVING: FAT FREE

*Note: "Nutritional analysis does not include cheese."

Nutritional Analysis Per Serving:

cal	g. fat	(%of cal)	g.fib	mg.chol	mg. sod
196	0.23	1	4.16	5	515

Rich/Poor?

Many of us have said, "That I have been rich and I have been poor and rich is better." There is some truth in lots of things that we say but sometimes we don't really think it through. If you talk to very many successful couples today that are having trouble in their marriages, they will talk about the good times when they first got married. Not much money. Eating lots of hot dogs and peanut butter. Going through hard times created a bonding. Difficult times have a way of bonding people together and building their characters. After you have everything (you think), you quit leaning on each other and start going your own way. Our walk with God tends to be that way. We tend to draw closer to God in hard times out of need. As things get better, we tend to not seek Him as much. I am not asking for difficulties but we need to seek Him and bless Him in the good times too!

CELERY AND MEAT CASSEROLE

1 6-ounce can tomato paste
8 ounces shredded fat free cheddar cheese
1 pound ground turkey breast
4 green peppers
1 button garlic
1 10 3/4- ounce can tomato soup
2 large onions
1 small bunch celery
1 package yokeless noodles
4 ounces mushrooms

METHOD:

Cook meat in Nonstick skillet.
Cook until lightly browned.
Pepper to taste.
Stir while cooking.
When meat is done, drain off all the grease and set aside.
Chop and saute onions, peppers, celery and garlic.
Stir well while cooking.
Pepper to taste.
Cook noodles in separate pot.
This is all of the cooking.
Mix the meat, cooked vegetables and noodles.
Add: 1 can tomato soup, 1 can tomato paste and 1 small can mushrooms (chopped fine).
Mix all together thoroughly, top sprinkle 8 ounces of fat free shredded cheese and put on top.
Put this in the oven until cheese melts and covers top.

SERVES: 6

FAT GRAMS PER SERVING: 2

Nutritional Analysis Per Serving:

cal	*g. fat*	*(%of cal)*	*g.fib*	*mg.chol*	*mg. sod*
611	*2.32*	*3*	*8.51*	*30*	*1776*

CHEESEBURGER CASSEROLE

1 pound lean ground sirloin
1/4 cup chopped onion
1 8-ounce can tomato sauce
1/2 cup catsup
8 ounces shredded fat free cheddar cheese
1 package low fat canned biscuits, cut in fourths with scissors

METHOD:

Brown meat and onions; drain.
Add tomato sauce and catsup to beef mixture.
Stir and place in casserole dish.
Sprinkle with grated cheese.
Top with biscuits and bake at 350 degrees for 15-20 minutes or until biscuits are golden brown.

Serves: 6

FAT GRAMS PER SERVING: 4

Nutritional Analysis Per Serving:

cal	*g. fat*	*(% of cal)*	*g.fib*	*mg. chol*	*mg. sod*
482	*3.98*	*7*	*1.96*	*56*	*2634*

CHEESE-PUFFED POTATO CASSEROLE

8 ounces fat free egg substitute
4 cups well-seasoned mashed potatoes
1 cup fat free shredded sharp Cheddar cheese
2 teaspoons finely chopped onion
2 teaspoons finely chopped green pepper
1/2 teaspoon celery salt
1/4 teaspoon paprika
2 tablespoon fat free margarine

METHOD:

Beat fat free egg substitute with mashed potatoes until well mixed.
Stir in cheese, margarine, onion, green pepper, celery salt.
Spoon lightly into a well-sprayed casserole dish (about 7x13 inches).
Sprinkle with paprika and bake in a moderately hot oven, 375 degrees for 25 minutes.

SERVES: 8

FAT GRAMS PER SERVING: FAT FREE

Nutritional Analysis Per Serving:

cal	*g. fat*	*(%of cal)*	*g.fib*	*mg.chol*	*mg. sod*
112	*0.50*	*4*	*0.03*	*3*	*484*

CHICKEN & BROCCOLI CASSEROLE

2	boneless, skinless chicken breasts
2	10-ounce packages frozen broccoli (chopped)
2	cans cream of chicken soup
1/2	cup fat free mayonnaise
1	teaspoon curry powder
3	ounces fat free croutons
1/2	teaspoon lemon juice

METHOD:

Boil chicken and cut into bite-size pieces when cool.
Cook broccoli and drain.
Make sauce using condensed soup, mayonnaise, curry powder and lemon juice.
In long baking dish, place layer of chicken, then broccoli and sauce.
Alternate in layers.
Place croutons on top.
Bake in 375 degree oven for 30 minutes.
Cook with foil over dish for 20 minutes to prevent topping from browning too fast.
SERVES: 6

FAT GRAMS PER SERVING: 8

Nutritional Analysis Per Serving:

cal	*g. fat*	*(% of cal)*	*g.fib*	*mg. chol*	*mg. sod*
253	*7.59*	*27*	*2.15*	*31*	*1151*

Bank

A bank is where we put our hard-earned money for safe keeping. We put valuables in our safety deposit boxes so no one can steal them.

The bank may hold title to our new home, car, boat, camper and to anything else we may hope to own.

The bank is where we put our treasure, but they are not fool-proof safe. Banks have gone under. Banks have been robbed. People have been cheated.

Where your treasure is, there will your heart be also.

CHICKEN GRAVY & BISCUITS

2 cups cooked, diced chicken breasts
1 10-ounce package frozen peas
1/2 cup cream of chicken soup
1 cup skim milk
1/2 cup FAT FREE sour cream
1/2 teaspoon salt
1/2 teaspoon pepper
1 1/4-cups shredded FAT FREE Cheddar cheese
1 can LOW FAT biscuits

METHOD:

Rinse peas under running water to separate.
Place in saucepan with rest of the ingredients, except biscuits, and heat to boiling.
Pour into a sprayed casserole dish and top with biscuits.
Bake in a 350-degree oven for about 20 minutes, or until biscuits are brown and casserole is bubbling.

SERVES: 6

FATS PER SERVING: 5

Nutritional Analysis Per Serving:

cal	*g. fat*	*(% of cal)*	*g.fib*	*mg. chol*	*mg. sod*
338	*5*	*13*	*4.56*	*51*	*868*

CHICKEN AND RICE CASSEROLE

1 cup rice (not cooked)
1/2 teaspoon celery seed
1/2 teaspoon oregano
1/2 teaspoon parsley flakes
1 can chicken and rice soup
1 can water
6 boneless, skinless chicken breasts

METHOD:

In a sprayed 2-quart casserole dish, add ingredients in order starting with the rice.
Put chicken into casserole dish with mixture, cover and cook at 350 degrees for two hours or until done.

SERVES: 6

FAT GRAMS PER SERVING: 1

Nutritional Analysis Per Serving:

cal	g. fat	(%of cal)	g.fib	mg.chol	mg. sod
171	1.43	8	0.28	17	354

CHICKEN CASSEROLE

1 cup chicken (cooked and cubed)
1 can cream chicken soup, condensed
3/4 cup fat free mayonnaise
1 cup diced celery
1 cup cooked rice
1 tablespoon grated onion
1 teaspoon lemon juice
1 small can water chestnuts
3 hard-boiled eggs, whites only
1 cup corn flakes
4 ounces fat free margarine, melted

METHOD:

Mix the above ingredients in large casserole dish. Put layer of eggs and top with cornflake crumbs. Bake 25 minutes at 350 degreees.

SERVES: 4

FAT GRAMS PER SERVING: 6

Nutritional Analysis Per Serving:

cal	*g. fat*	*(% of cal)*	*g.fib*	*mg. chol*	*mg. sod*
320	*6.40*	*18*	*3.96*	*38*	*1340*

CHICKEN OR TURKEY CASSEROLE

2 cups chopped chicken or turkey breast
1 cup cooked rice
3/4 cup fat free mayonnaise
1 teaspoon lemon juice
1 can Healthy Request cream of chicken
2 hard-boiled egg whites, chopped
1 cup celery
1 small onion
1 small can water chestnuts
1 small can mushrooms
1/4 cup cup fat free margarine
10 slices fat free bread

METHOD:

Crumble bread into crumbs.
Mix melted margarine lightly over crumbs.
Put ingredients in casserole dish and top with buttered crumbs.
Bake at 350 degrees for 45 minutes.

SERVES: 10

FAT GRAMS PER SERVING: 2

Nutritional Analysis Per Serving:

cal	*g. fat*	*(%of cal)*	*g.fib*	*mg.chol*	*mg. sod*
220	*2.07*	*8*	*4.15*	*20*	*605*

CHICKEN SALAD CASSEROLE

1 cup boneless skinless chicken breast, cooked and cubed
1 cup celery, chopped
1 teaspoon chopped onion
2 boiled egg whites
1 can of cream of chicken soup
1/2 cup fat free salad dressing

METHOD:

Combine the ingredients and put into a casserole dish. Bake at 350 degrees for 20-25 minutes.

SERVES: 4

FAT GRAMS PER SERVING: 6

Nutritional Analysis Per Serving:

cal	*g. fat*	*(% of cal)*	*g.fib*	*mg. chol*	*mg. sod*
180	*6.24*	*31*	*0 .68*	*38*	*896*

CHICKEN SPAGHETTI CASSEROLE

3 boneless skinless chicken breasts, cooked and diced
3 cups cooked spaghetti
1 10-1/2-ounce can mushroom soup
1/4 teaspoon Worcestershire sauce
1 2-ounce can pimento
1/2 10-ounce bottle catsup
3 medium onions
1 bell pepper
1 stalk celery
1 8-ounce package shredded fat free cheese

METHOD:

Boil onions, celery and pepper together.
Cook spaghetti; drain and add to chicken; add celery, onions, pepper, pimento and soup to spaghetti.
Grate cheese and add with Worcestershire sauce and catsup.
Mix together and salt to taste.
Save a little grated cheese to sprinkle on top.
Bake until brown.

SERVES: 8

FAT GRAMS PER SERVING: 4

Nutritional Analysis Per Serving:

cal	g. fat	(%of cal)	g.fib	mg.chol	mg. sod
369	3.62	9	1.64	22	1709

CHICKEN-POTATO CASSEROLE

6 boneless skinless chicken breasts, cut up
4 cups potatoes (thinly sliced and peeled)
4 medium onions
1 large can evaporated skim milk
2 slices bacon
2 tablespoons fat free margarine
1/4 teaspoon salt
1/4 teaspoon pepper
1 teaspoon ground thyme
1 teaspoon paprika

METHOD:

Put potatoes and sliced onions in large roasting pan and sprinkle with salt, pepper and thyme.
Add 1/2 cup hot water to pan.
Reserve 1/4 cup milk and pour remainder over vegetables.
Put in 400 degree oven while preparing chicken.
In skillet, cook bacon until browned.
Remove and drain.
Add margarine to skillet, then add chicken and brown on all sides, removing pieces as they brown.
Put chicken in pan with potatoes and sprinkle with seasoning.
Crumble bacon and sprinkle over top.
Cover tightly with foil and bake in 400 degree oven 1 hour. Uncover and pour reserved milk on top and sprinkle with paprika. Bake 30 minutes or until meat is done.

SERVES: 8

FAT GRAMS PER SERVING: 3

Nutritional Analysis Per Serving:

cal	*g. fat*	*(% of cal)*	*g.fib*	*mg. chol*	*mg. sod*
221	*3.28*	*13*	*1.23*	*55*	*246*

If Looks Could?

If looks could kill, I would be dead. What did you mean by that look?

Our looks or expressions say a whole lot more than our words do sometimes. We need to be careful about the way we look a well as what we say.

Once again, it is the way we live our daily lives that speaks a whole lot more than our words.

You may be doing something for a neighbor because it is the Christian thing to do, but if your actions indicate that you are only doing it because you have to, it can turn out to be a negative witness.

Do a good deed for someone.

If we did the deed in love, our face and actions will show it.

When people say they can read you like a book, they are talking about the way you look and act. If looks could, what would yours say?

CHUNKY CASSEROLE

2 tablespoons fat free margarine
1/2 cup chopped onions
1/2 cup chopped canned tomatoes
1/2 cup shredded fat free cheddar cheese
1/2 pound Mr. Turkey polish sausage
1 19-ounce can chunky split pea soup
1 cup cooked elbow macaroni

METHOD:

In pan melt margarine and add sliced sausage.
Then add onion.
Saute until tender.
Add soup, tomatoes and macaroni.
Pour into one quart casserole and bake in 350 degree oven for 25 minutes or until meat is done.
Stir.
Top with shredded cheese and bake five more minutes, or until cheese melts.

SERVES: 6

FAT GRAMS PER SERVING: 2

Nutritional Analysis Per Serving:

cal	*g. fat*	*(% of cal)*	*g.fib*	*mg. chol*	*mg. sod*
163	*1.94*	*11*	*2.53*	*20*	*693*

CORN AND RICE CASSEROLE

3 cups cooked rice
1/4 cup minced onion
1-1/2 cup skim milk
1/4 teaspoon pepper
1 10-ounce package frozen corn
2 cups shredded fat free Cheddar cheese
1/4 teaspoon paprika

METHOD:

In bowl combine rice, thawed corn, onion, cheese, milk, and pepper.
Mix well and pour into sprayed 2 quart casserole dish.
Sprinkle with paprika.
Bake in 350 degree oven for 40-45 minutes or until knife inserted in center comes out clean.

SERVES: 6

FAT GRAMS PER SERVING: 1

Nutritional Analysis Per Serving:

cal	*g. fat*	*(%of cal)*	*g.fib*	*mg.chol*	*mg. sod*
248	*0.98*	*4*	*2.90*	*6*	*330*

CORN CASSEROLE

1/2 cup chopped onions
1/2 cup green peppers
1/2 cup celery
2 teaspoons garlic powder
2 8-ounce cans tomato sauce
1 pound ground turkey breast
2 tablespoons chili powder or 2 teaspoons hot sauce
1 pound frozen niblet corn with juice
1 pound fat free block cheese, grated
8 ounce package yokeless noodles

METHOD:

Saute onions, peppers, celery, and garlic powder on low heat.
Brown ground meat and chili powder.
Cook noodles according to package directions.
Mix noodles, corn and cheese with other ingredients.
Bake 30 minutes at 350 degrees.

SERVES: 10

FAT GRAMS PER SERVING: 1

Nutritional Analysis Per Serving:

cal	*g. fat*	*(% of cal)*	*g.fib*	*mg. chol*	*mg. sod*
262	*1.14*	*3*	*3.59*	*12*	*1212*

CORNBREAD CASSEROLE

1 box Jiffy cornbread mix
1 cup chopped celery
1 cup chopped green peppers
1/2 cup chopped onions
2 cups fat free mayonnaise
2 tablespoons sugar
1/2 pound crisp/drained turkey bacon

METHOD:

Prepare cornbread as directed using skim milk, fat free egg substitute to replace egg.
Bake cornbread; crumble and set aside.
Mix all other ingredients together.
Layer in dish alternating half the ingredients and half the cornbread until all is used.
Refrigerate 3 hours before serving.

SERVES: 8

FAT GRAMS PER SERVING: 6

Nutritional Analysis Per Serving:

cal	*g. fat*	*(%of cal)*	*g.fib*	*mg.chol*	*mg. sod*
223	*5.63*	*23*	*1.60*	*10*	*1003*

CORN FLAKES SWEET POTATO CASSEROLE

1 pound sweet potatoes
1 cup sugar
1 teaspoon cinnamon
1 cup evaporated skim milk
8 ounces fat free margarine (promise)
4 ounces egg substitute
1 cup skim milk
1-1/2 cup evaporated skim milk

TOPPING:

1 cup corn flake crumbs
1/2 cup sugar, brown

METHOD:

Mix together, put into sprayed dish.

TOP METHOD:

Rub above ingredients together and sprinkle over sweet potatoes. Bake at 350 degrees for 30 minutes.

SERVES: 6

FAT GRAMS PER SERVING; FAT FREE

WATCH THOSE CALORIES!

Nutritional Analysis Per Serving:

cal	*g. fat*	*(% of cal)*	*g.fib*	*mg. chol*	*mg. sod*
316	*0.45*	*1*	*1.61*	*5*	*583*

CORNY BEEF CASSEROLE

1 pound lean ground sirloin
1/2 cup diced green pepper
1/2 cup chopped onion
15 ounce can dark red kidney beans
8 ounce can tomato sauce
1/4 teaspoon garlic powder
1 eight and one half ounce package Jiffy corn muffin mix
1/3 cup skim milk
2 ounces fat free egg substitute
1/2 cup shredded fat free Cheddar cheese

METHOD:

Brown sirloin, green pepper and onion in a skillet; drain excess fat.
Stir in kidney beans, tomato sauce, and garlic powder.
Spread mixture into sprayed 9-inch square pan.
Prepare muffin mix according to package directions; add 1/3 cup skim milk , 2 ounces egg beater; stir in cheese.
Spread batter over meat mixture; bake in preheated 375 degree oven 30 to 35 minutes.

SERVES: 8

FAT GRAMS PER SERVING: 6

Nutritional Analysis Per Serving:

cal	g. fat	(%of cal)	g.fib	mg.chol	mg. sod
348	5.60	14	3.04	27	1116

Relax

A spirit of fear? Who wants that?Love, peace and a sound mind? We all want these.

Worried about what may happen tomorrow? The Good Book says not to worry about tomorrow because tomorrow has enough problems of its own.

Most of the things we worry about don't come to pass anyway. Ever hear of "The Serenity Prayer"?

GOD, grant me the *Serenity* to accept the things I cannot change;

Courage to change the things I can; and

Wisdom to know the difference.

Do you get the idea that God is telling us to "Relax"? Just a little bit?

CRUNCH TOP CASSEROLE

2 cups cooked boneless skinless chicken breast
8 ounces cream of chicken soup
2 tablespoons fat free Parmesan cheese
1/2 teaspoon oregano
Dash garlic powder
2/3 cup skim milk
2 tablespoons instant minced onion
Dash pepper
2 cups sliced zucchini
1 1/3 cups uncooked oats
1/2 cup fat free margarine
1/2 teaspoon thyme

METHOD:

In pan combine soup, milk, cheese, onion, garlic powder and pepper.
Mix well and bring to boil.
Stir in chicken and zucchini.
Spoon mixture into 11x7-inch baking dish.
In bowl combine oats, melted margarine, oregano, and thyme.
Mix well and sprinkle evenly over casserole.
Bake in 375 degree oven for about 25 minutes, or until topping is golden brown.

SERVES: 6

FAT GRAMS PER SERVING: 4

Nutritional Analysis Per Serving:

cal	*g. fat*	*(%of cal)*	*g.fib*	*mg.chol*	*mg. sod*
145	*3.69*	*23*	*2.24*	*8*	*432*

DELIGHTFUL SQUASH CASSEROLE

8 medium yellow squash
4 slices turkey bacon
1 small onion, chopped
2 ounces fat free egg substitute, beaten
1 cup shredded fat free Cheddar cheese
1/4 teaspoon salt and 1/4 teaspoon pepper to taste
1 tablespoon Worcestershire sauce

METHOD:

Cook squash in a small amount of boiling, salted water until tender; drain well and mash.
Cook bacon until it is crisp; drain well and crumble, reserving the drippings.
Saute onion in drippings, then combine all ingredients.
Stir mixture well.

SERVES: 6

FATS GRAMS PER SERVING: 4

Nutritional Analysis Per Serving:

cal	*g. fat*	*(% of cal)*	*g.fib*	*mg. chol*	*mg. sod*
320	*4.26*	*12*	*23.56*	*9*	*395*

EASY CASSEROLE

1 pound ground turkey breast
1 can Spanish rice
1/4 cup catsup
1/2 cup fat free grated cheese

METHOD:

Brown and cook meat in Nonstick skillet; drain.
Add Spanish rice and catsup.
Top with grated cheese and put in 350 degree oven until bubbling hot.

SERVES: 4

FAT GRAMS PER SERVING: 2

Nutritional Analysis Per Serving:

cal	*g. fat*	*(%of cal)*	*g.fib*	*mg.chol*	*mg. sod*
170	*1.54*	*8*	*1.83*	*15*	*1220*

FIVE SOUP CASSEROLE

4 ounces fat free margarine
1 3/4 cups dry Minute Rice
6 boneless skinless chicken breasts
1 can cream of celery soup
1 can cream of chicken soup
1 can cream of mushroom soup
1 can onion soup
1 can beef consomme
1/2 cup fat free Parmesan cheese

METHOD:

Melt margarine and add rice.
Place chicken on bed of rice in covered baking dish.
Blend together the five soups.
Pour over chicken and rice.
Coat with Parmesan cheese.
Cover and bake three hours in 275 degree oven or until chicken is done.

SERVES: 12

FAT GRAMS PER SERVING: 6

Nutritional Analysis Per Serving:

cal	*g. fat*	*(% of cal)*	*g.fib*	*mg. chol*	*mg. sod*
235	*6.47*	*25*	*0.68*	*41*	*1374*

GARDEN PATCH MACARONI CASSEROLE

7 ounce package elbow macaroni
2 quarts coarsely shredded cabbage
1 cup cooked sliced carrots
1 cup cooked peas
1 can cream of mushroom soup
1 tablespoon chopped chives
2 cups fat free sour cream
1 cup shredded fat free American cheese

METHOD:

Cook macaroni in boiling water until just tender and drain.
Cook the cabbage in boiling water 6 or 7 minutes or until just tender-crisp and drain.
Add the macaroni, carrot slices, peas, and chives. Mix the soup and sour cream together and fold into macaroni mixture.
Mix well.
Place in a greased 2 1/2-quart baking dish and sprinkle with cheese.
Bake at 350 degrees for 25 to 30 minutes or until heated through and cheese is melted.

SERVES: 8

FAT GRAMS PER SERVING: 4

Nutritional Analysis Per Serving:

cal	*g. fat*	*(%of cal)*	*g.fib*	*mg.chol*	*mg. sod*
367	*4.01*	*10*	*2.67*	*10*	*548*

GOURMET POTATO CASSEROLE

6 medium potatoes
2 cups fat free shredded cheese
1/2 cup fat free margarine
1/2 cup fat free sour cream
1/3 cup green onions
1/2 teaspoon pepper
2 tablespoons fat free margarine (for dabbing)
1/4 teaspoon paprika

METHOD:

Boil potatoes and mash.
In saucepan over low heat combine cheese, green onions and margarine; stir until melted.
Blend sour cream and pepper
Fold in with potatoes.
Bake in a 2 to 4-quart dish, then dab with margarine and paprika. Bake at 350 degrees for 30 minutes.

SERVES: 10

FAT GRAMS PER SERVING: FAT FREE

Nutritional Analysis Per Serving:

cal	*g. fat*	*(% of cal)*	*g.fib*	*mg. chol*	*mg. sod*
142	*0.12*	*1*	*1.81*	*5*	*283*

Super Glue?

In the Good Book , we see faith as a substance in some translations.

Faith is as real as any fear that you have. Fear can keep you from doing many things and fear can make you do many things. Faith should be the same way.

Our faith should be like a super glue. It should hold us so close to God and His Word that nothing can separate us. "Nothing can separate us from God's love."

We need to be that way with God. No matter what others say. No matter what the situation or tribulation, nothing should separate us from what God has said and our love for Him.

The faith is the super glue that holds us together in all things so that we don't fall apart. It keeps us close to God while He is causing all things to work together for our good.

There is glue, special glue and there is super glue. God's Word says that there is faith, little faith, and great (super) faith. Get the best.

GROUND TURKEY CASSEROLE

8 ounce package yokeless noodles
1 green pepper (chopped)
1 10 3/4-ounce can mushroom soup
1 small can pimento
2 large onions (chopped)
1 1/2 pounds ground turkey breast
1 10 3/4-ounce can tomato soup
1/2 pound fat free shredded cheddar cheese

METHOD:

Cook noodles until tender; drain.
Cook meat, onions and pepper a short time.
Add mushroom soup, can of water, tomato soup and chopped pimento if desired to decorate top of casserole.
Make two layers each, alternating noodles, then meat mixture and grated cheese.
Bake at 350 degrees for 30 minutes.

SERVES: 10

FAT GRAMS PER SERVING: 3

Nutritional Analysis Per Serving:

cal	*g. fat*	*(% of cal)*	*g.fib*	*mg. chol*	*mg. sod*
306	*3.23*	*9*	*1.42*	*21*	*1178*

HAM CASSEROLE

3 cups cooked green beans
1 10 3/4-ounce can cream of mushroom soup
1 small can evaporated skim milk
2 cups diced 95% lean cooked ham
3/4 cup fat free shredded cheddar cheese
1 teaspoon pepper
1 teaspoon paprika

METHOD:

In sprayed shallow dish put drained beans.
Top with ham.
Combine soup, milk, cheese and pepper.
Cook and stir over medium heat until thickened and cheese has melted.
Pour over casserole.
Sprinkle with paprika.
Bake in 350 degree oven for 20 to 25 minutes or until bubbly.

SERVES: 6

FAT GRAMS PER SERVING: 7

Nutritional Analysis Per Serving:

cal	*g. fat*	*(%of cal)*	*g.fib*	*mg.chol*	*mg. sod*
198	*6.79*	*31*	*1.78*	*50*	*1250*

HAMBURGER CASSEROLE

Use fat free cornbread recipe on page 25.

1 pound ground turkey breast
1/2 pound shredded fat free cheese
1 can corn
1 cup onion, chopped

METHOD:

Brown meat and onion; drain off excess fat.
Add 1/2 can corn and 1/2 cup cheese.
Place on heat until cheese melts.
Mix cornbread according to directions.
Add 1/2 can corn to batter.
Place 1/2 batter in sprayed Nonstick skillet; add 1/2 meat mixture, rest of cornbread mixture and remaining meat mixture. Bake as directed on cornbread recipe.

SERVES: 4

FAT GRAMS PER SERVING: 4

Nutritional Analysis Per Serving:

cal	*g. fat*	*(% of cal)*	*g.fib*	*mg. chol*	*mg. sod*
287	*3.61*	*11*	*2.29*	*38*	*789*

HAMBURGER-NOODLE CASSEROLE

1 onion, peeled and chopped
1 pound lean ground sirloin
1 10-1/2-ounce can tomato soup
1 cup water
1/2 8-ounce package yokeless noodles, uncooked
1/4 teaspoon pepper to taste
2 1/2 cups cream-style canned corn
1 cup sliced mushrooms
1 cup shredded fat free cheese

METHOD:

In a sprayed Nonstick skillet saute onion until tender.
Add meat; cook until meat is no longer pink.
Drain meat.
Add tomato soup, water and noodles; cook until noodles are tender.
Season to taste with pepper.
Add corn and mushrooms; stir.
Top with cheese; bake in preheated 350 degree oven 45 minutes.

SERVES: 6

FAT GRAMS PER SERVING: 4

Nutritional Analysis Per Serving:

cal	*g. fat*	*(%of cal)*	*g.fib*	*mg.chol*	*mg. sod*
287	*3.61*	*11*	*2.29*	*38*	*789*

LIMA BEAN AND BROCCOLI CASSEROLE

1 package frozen lima beans, cooked and drained
1 package frozen broccoli, cooked and drained
1 10 3/4 ounce can cream of mushroom soup
1 package onion soup mix
1 cup fat free sour cream
3 cups Rice Krispies
3 tablespoon fat free margarine

METHOD:

Mix all ingredients together, except Rice Krispies.
Bake at 350 degrees for 30 minutes.
Brown Rice Krispies in 3 tablespoons fat free margarine.
Put on top of casserole and serve.

SERVES: 8

FAT GRAMS PER SERVING: 3

Nutritional Analysis Per Serving:

cal	g. fat	(% of cal)	g.fib	mg. chol	mg. sod
234	3.30	13	5.07	4	1166

It's Hard

When you are waiting on God, it isn't easy. It is hard!

As a matter of fact, many things we do by ourselves seem like they are impossible. However, The Good Book says that with Him, all things are possible.

Waiting takes so long, I guess that is why it is called waiting. If you aren't doing anything, it even seems to take longer.

The opposite of doing nothing is the way to make the time go faster.

Find things to do. Ask God to show you. He wants to help.

He doesn't want us to be lazy. The Word has a lot to say about being lazy. It is all for our own good.

When God shows you something to do and opens the door, be ready to go or do.

As you do what He provides, if you truly get involved, the time will go by much faster and sometimes the answer even seems to come quicker.

MACARONI CASSEROLE

1 pound ground turkey breast (cooked)
1 1-1/2-ounce package Sloppy Joe seasoning mix
1 6-ounce can tomato paste
1 1/4 cup water
2 cups macaroni
1 pound frozen package whole kernel corn,
2 cups shredded fat free sharp Cheddar cheese

METHOD:

Prepare first four ingredients as directed on Sloppy Joe seasoning mix package.
Cook macaroni in boiling water until just tender; drain.
Stir in meat mixture, corn and 1 cup cheese.
Turn into sprayed 2-quart casserole dish.
Sprinkle with remaining cheese.
Bake, uncovered, in 350 degree oven until hot, about 45 minutes.

SERVES: 8

FAT GRAMS PER SERVING: 2

Nutritional Analysis Per Serving:

cal	*g. fat*	*(% of cal)*	*g.fib*	*mg. chol*	*mg. sod*
301	*1.70*	*5*	*2.57*	*10*	*327*

MEAT & POTATO CASSEROLE

1 pound turkey breast
2 cans green beans, drained
1 cup diced onion
1/2 cup diced green pepper
1 cup frozen whole corn
1 can tomato soup
1/4 teaspoon pepper
2 cups instant potatoes, creamed

METHOD:

Cook meat in sprayed Nonstick skillet.
Saute onions and green peppers in microwave until tender.
Add to meat.
Cook until meat is done.
Remove from heat.
Add remaining ingredients, except potatoes.
Spread potatoes on top.
Bake at 350 degrees for 45 minutes.

SERVES: 8

FAT GRAMS PER SERVING: 6

Nutritional Analysis Per Serving:

cal	*g. fat*	*(%of cal)*	*g.fib*	*mg.chol*	*mg. sod*
858	*6.42*	*7*	*0.75*	*8*	*436*

MUSHROOM CASSEROLE

1 pound ground turkey breast
6 medium potatoes
1/2 can cream of mushroom soup
4 slices fat free American cheese
1/2 can water

METHOD:

Brown meat and add seasonings.
Slice potatoes.
Layer each ingredient in casserole dish and top with mushroom soup.
Bake at 350 degrees for 1 hour or until potatoes are done.

SERVES: 6

FAT GRAMS PER SERVING: 2

Nutritional Analysis Per Serving:

cal	g. fat	(% of cal)	g.fib	mg. chol	mg. sod
188	2.19	10	2.64	12	423

PEA CASSEROLE

4 ounces cooked yokeless noodles
1 pound ground turkey breast
8 ounces mushroom soup
8 ounces tomato soup
1 pound frozen peas

METHOD:

Brown ground meat in Nonstick skillet until done.
Mix mushroom soup, tomato soup, noodles and peas in baking dish, adding it to the meat.
Mixed vegetables may be substituted for peas.
Cover and bake at 350 degrees for 1 hour or until hot.

SERVES: 6

FAT GRAMS PER SERVING: 4

Nutritional Analysis Per Serving:

cal	*g. fat*	*(%of cal)*	*g.fib*	*mg.chol*	*mg. sod*
268	*4.29*	*14*	*8.39*	*9*	*761*

PORK CHOP CASSEROLE

6 4-ounce lean boneless pork chops
1/2 can cream of mushroom soup
1 can onion soup
1 small can mushroom steak sauce
2 cups raw rice
1 1/2 can of water

METHOD:

Mix all these ingredients together, except pork chops. Cover and brown pork chops and add to the mixture. Cook in oven at 350 degrees for 1 1/2 hours.

SERVES: 6

FAT GRAMS PER SERVING: 11

Nutritional Analysis Per Serving:

cal	*g. fat*	*(% of cal)*	*g.fib*	*mg. chol*	*mg. sod*
508	*10.68*	*19*	*0.50*	*72*	*1396*

RICE CASSEROLE

1 pound ground turkey breast
1 small onion, sliced very thin
1/2 cup diced celery
1 teaspoon soy sauce
1/8 teaspoon oregano
8 ounces condensed cream of chicken soup
1 cup cooked rice

METHOD:

In Nonstick skillet, cook turkey discarding fat.
Combine all ingredients except rice in crock pot.
Cook on high 3 hours.
Add cooked rice.

SERVES: 6

FAT GRAMS PER SERVING: 2

Nutritional Analysis Per Serving:

cal	*g. fat*	*(%of cal)*	*g.fib*	*mg.chol*	*mg. sod*
100	*2.45*	*22*	*1.05*	*12*	*492*

RICELAND RICE CASSEROLE

1 1/2 pounds ground turkey breast
1 medium onion, chopped
1 bell pepper, chopped
1 can cream of mushroom soup
16 ounce frozen package whole kernel corn
2 cups cooked Riceland extra long grain rice
1 can Ro-Tel tomatoes
1 small can mushrooms, sliced
1 cup shredded fat free Cheddar cheese

METHOD:

Saute meat, chopped onion and bell pepper.
Add all remaining ingredients, except cheese; simmer 50 minutes. Pour into greased casserole dish.
Top with shredded cheese.
Bake at 325 degrees until cheese melts and is slightly browned.

SERVES: 6

FAT GRAMS PER SERVING: 5

Nutritional Analysis Per Serving:

cal	*g. fat*	*(% of cal)*	*g.fib*	*mg. chol*	*mg. sod*
331	*5.32*	*14*	*2.12*	*16*	*886*

SAUSAGE CASSEROLE

2 pounds Mr. Turkey polish sausage
1 pound package frozen corn
1 can tomato soup
1 can mushroom soup
3/4 pound large yokeless noodles
16 ounces fat free mild Cheddar cheese
1 green pepper (chopped and saute)
1 large onion (chopped and saute)

METHOD:

Cut sausage in pepperoni slices and cook.
Season with pepper to taste.
Cook noodles until tender in salted water.
Don't over cook.
Grate the cheese and divide in half.
Mix all ingredients together except for half of cheese.
Pour into extra large casserole dish.
Sprinkle with remaining cheese.
Bake 30 minutes at 300 degrees.

SERVES: 13

FAT GRAMS PER SERVING: 4

Nutritional Analysis Per Serving:

cal	*g. fat*	*(%of cal)*	*g.fib*	*mg.chol*	*mg. sod*
485	*4.29*	*7*	*1.95*	*43*	*1977*

SHIRRED POTATO CARROT CASSEROLE

2 tablespoons fat free margarine
1 1/2 tablespoons flour
1 teaspoon salt
2 cups skim milk
1 cup shredded raw carrots
2 cups shredded raw potatoes
1 tablespoon grated onion

METHOD:

In a saucepan, melt margarine over medium heat.
Blend in flour and salt.
Remove from heat and graduallly blend in milk.
Cook until thickened.
Mix in potatoes, carrots and onion.
Pour into bakin dish.
Bake 1 1/2 hours in --- shallow 1 1/2 quart casserole at 325 degrees.
Sprinkle fat free cheese on top and bake 30 minutes longer.

SERVES: 4

FAT GRAMS PER SERVING: FAT FREE

*NOTE: "Below analysis does NOT include cheese."

Nutritional Analysis Per Serving:

cal	*g. fat*	*(% of cal)*	*g.fib*	*mg. chol*	*mg. sod*
125	*0.35*	*3*	*1.95*	*2*	*314*

SEAFOOD CASSEROLE

1 can (3 ounce) sliced mushrooms
1/4 cup flour
2 (7 1/2-ounce) cans Light water packed tuna
1/4 cup chopped onion
1/4 cup fat free margarine
11/4 cup skim milk
1 cup shredded fat free cheddar cheese
1/2 cup cornflake crumbs

METHOD:

Drain mushrooms and reserve broth.
In pan melt margarine and blend in flour.
Add enough milk to reserved broth to make two cups.
Stir milk into flour and cook over medium heat until thickened, stirring constantly.
Add drained tuna, mushrooms, cheese and chopped onion.
Heat and pour into sprayed 1 1/2 quart casserole dish.
Top with crumbs and bake in 350 degree oven for 30 to 40 minutes.

SERVES: 4

FAT GRAMS PER SERVING: 1

Nutritional Analysis Per Serving:

cal	*g. fat*	*(%of cal)*	*g.fib*	*mg.chol*	*mg. sod*
253	*1.20*	*4*	*1.21*	*62*	*1025*

SOUTH OF THE BORDER CASSEROLE

1 pound ground turkey breast
1 medium onion, chopped
1/2 cup chopped celery
2 1-pound cans chili beans
1 16-ounce can tomato sauce
1 cup shredded fat free Cheddar cheese
1 1/2 teaspoons chili powder
1/4 teaspoon oregano
1 cup water

METHOD:

In Nonstick skillet, cook turkey, discarding fat. Combine all ingredients in slow cooker, stirring well. Cook on low 4-6 hours.

SERVES: 8

FAT GRAMS PER SERVING: 2

Nutritional Analysis Per Serving:

cal	*g. fat*	*(% of cal)*	*g.fib*	*mg. chol*	*mg. sod*
293	*2.10*	*6*	*12.90*	*8*	*1665*

SQUASH CASSEROLE

2 ounces fat free egg substitute
1/2 onion, chopped
1 10-3/4-ounce can cream of mushroom soup
1/2 cup softened fat free margarine
1/2 cup fat free Italian bread crumbs,
buttered with fat free margarine
2 cups cooked squash, well drained
Season

METHOD:

Combine all ingredients except bread crumbs.
Pour in sprayed casserole dish and top with bread crumbs.
Bake in 350 degree oven for 30 minutes or until hot and bubbly.

SERVES: 4

FAT GRAMS PER SERVING: 7

Nutritional Analysis Per Serving:

cal	g. fat	(%of cal)	g.fib	mg.chol	mg. sod
192	6.90	32	2.49	1	1130

SQUASH CASSEROLE - 2

1 1/2 cups cooked butternut squash
1 tablespoon squash
1 tablespoon flour
1/2 teaspoon ginger
1/2 teaspoon cinnamon
2 cups skim milk
3/4 cup sugar
1/2 teaspoon salt
1/2 teaspoon nutmeg
8 ounces fat free egg substitute

METHOD:

Heat milk and squash together.
In a bowl, combine sugar, flour, salt and spices.
Add a bit of milk and squash to the fat free egg substitute and mix together, then add remainder of milk and squash and mix with egg beater.
Pour into 8-inch pie pan and bake at 400 degrees for 15 minutes or until done.

SERVES: 4

FAT GRAMS PER SERVING: 2

Nutritional Analysis Per Serving:

cal	*g. fat*	*(% of cal)*	*g.fib*	*mg. chol*	*mg. sod*
611	*2.32*	*3*	*8.51*	*30*	*1776*

NOODLE CASSEROLE

1 pound ground turkey breast
1 medium onion, sliced very thin
1 1/2 teaspoons salt
1/8 teaspoon pepper
1 teaspoon Worchestershire sauce
8 ounces condensed cream of celery soup
1 soup can water
1 1-pound can cream-style corn
2 cups (about half an 8-ounce package) eggless noodles

METHOD:

In Nonstick skillet brown turkey, discarding fat.
Combine all ingredients except noodles in cooker.
Cook on high 3 hours.
Add noodles and cook until done (about 15 minutes).

SERVES: 4

FAT GRAMS PER SERVING: 3

Nutritional Analysis Per Serving:

cal	*g. fat*	*(%of cal)*	*g.fib*	*mg.chol*	*mg. sod*
261	*3.07*	*11*	*2.77*	*13*	*321*

SWISS 'N CHICKEN CASSEROLE

4 cups chopped, cooked boneless skinless chicken breast
2 cups diced celery
2 cups croutons
8 fat free Swiss cheese
1 cup fat free Miracle Whip
1/2 cup skim milk
1/4 cup chopped onion
1/4 teaspoon pepper

METHOD:

Heat oven to 350 degrees.
Mix all ingredients.
Spoon into 2-quart casserole dish.
Bake 40 minutes or until thoroughly heated.

Serves: 8

FAT GRAMS PER SERVING: 4

Nutritional Analysis Per Serving:

cal	*g. fat*	*(% of cal)*	*g.fib*	*mg. chol*	*mg. sod*
239	*3.49*	*13*	*0.59*	*65*	*659*

NOTES

TEXAS CASSEROLE

1 pound dried pinto beans
4 large onions, chopped
1 pound lean ground sirloin
1 teaspoon whole or ground cumin
1 1/2 tablespoons oregano
2 1/2 cups water
1 1/4 pounds tomatoes
4 cloves garlic, minced
2 tablespoons chili powder
1 teaspoon red pepper

METHOD:

Wash and drain beans in fresh water.
Simmer beans until tender.
Saute onions in microwave until golden color.
Add ground sirloin, then brown.
Boil cumin and oregano in water.
Strain seasoned water into meat.
Mash tomatoes well with fork; add with garlic to meat.
Add chili powder, red pepper.
Add to beans; simmer one hour.

SERVES: 6

FAT GRAMS PER SERVING: 4

Nutritional Analysis Per Serving:

cal	*g. fat*	*(% of cal)*	*g.fib*	*mg. chol*	*mg. sod*
266	*3.72*	*13*	*6.74*	*35*	*426*

TURKEY CHEESE CASSEROLE

8 ounce package yokeless noodles
12 slices cooked turkey
4 large onions, chopped
1/2 teaspoon crumbled tarragon
1/2 pound shredded fat free cheese
1/2 cup fat free margarine
1 clove garlic, minced
2 cups condensed evaporated skim milk
1 cup crushed fat free dry bread crumbs
1 cup water

METHOD:

Cook noodles in water until tender.
Drain and pour into bowl.
Toss with cheese until noodles are coated with cheese.
Pour into buttered (with Fat free margarine) 2-quart casserole dish.
Top with turkey slices.
In skillet heat margarine and saute onion and garlic until transparent.
Pour onion mixture into food processor or blender, add water.
Whirl until smooth.
Pour back into sauce and stir in milk and tarragon.
Stir over low heat until mixture thickens, about 10 minutes. Pour over turkey and sprinkle with crumbs.
Bake in 350 degree oven for 35 to 40 minutes.

SERVES: 8

FAT GRAMS PER SERVING: 1

Nutritional Analysis Per Serving:

cal	*g. fat*	*(%of cal)*	*g.fib*	*mg.chol*	*mg. sod*
443	*1.42*	*2*	*2.51*	*25*	*1300*

Quotes for the Day

Fear is the darkroom where negatives are developed.

--e.l.

If you're yearning for the good old days, just turn off the air conditioning.

--griff niblack

The closest to perfection a person ever comes is when he fills out a job application form.

--Stanley J. Randall

TURNIP CASSEROLE

6 cups mashed turnips
8 ounce package fat free cream cheese
1/4 cup sugar
12 ounce fat free tub margarine
5 slices fat free bread crumbs, buttered with fat free margarine

METHOD:

Cook enough turnips to make 6 cups of mashed turnips.
Drain and mash.
Add softened cream cheese, sugar and margarine and mix well.
Pour into casserole and top with bread crumbs.
Bake in 350 degree oven until bubbly hot and lightly browned.

Note: Rutabagas or carrots (not included in below nutritional analysis) may also be used in this recipe. For a Christmas effect, pimento strips in the form of a poinsettia add a nice effect on top of the crumbs.

SERVES: 10

FAT GRAMS PER SERVING: FAT FREE

Nutritional Analysis Per Serving:

cal	*g. fat*	*(%of cal)*	*g.fib*	*mg.chol*	*mg. sod*
143	*0.27*	*2*	*2.94*	*3*	*575*

WESTERN-STYLE CASSEROLE

1 pound lean ground sirloin
1/4 cup chopped onion
1 pound frozen package whole kernel corn
1 16-ounce can red kidney beans, drained
1 10 3/4-ounce can condensed tomato soup
1 cup shredded fat free Cheddar cheese
1/4 cup dark corn syrup
1/4 skim milk
1 tablespoon chili powder
1 cup Lite biscuit baking mix

METHOD:

Cook sirloin and onion in a large skillet over medium heat 5 minutes, or until browned.
Drain well.
Stir in corn, beans, soup, cheese, corn syrup, 1/4 cup milk and chili powder.
Spoon mixture into a 2-quart casserole dish.
Bake in preheated 450 degree oven 20 to 25 minutes, or until bubbly.
Beat baking mix and 1/3 cup milk with a fork in medium-size bowl until blended.
(Mixture will be thick.)
Drop mixture by spoonfuls on top of meat mixture; bake in preheated 400 degree oven 25 minutes, or until biscuits are golden.

SERVES: 8

FAT GRAMS PER SERVING: 5

Nutritional Analysis Per Serving:

cal	*g. fat*	*(% of cal)*	*g.fib*	*mg. chol*	*mg. sod*
484	*4.88*	*9*	*2.32*	*28*	*1068*

ZUCCHINI CASSEROLE

1 red onion, sliced
1 green pepper, cut in thin strips
4 medium zucchini (scrubbed but not peeled), sliced
1 10-ounce can tomatoes
1 cup chopped parsley
1 teaspoon salt
1/2 teaspoon pepper
1/2 teaspoon basil
1 tablespoon fat free margarine
1/4 cup grated fat free Parmesan cheese

METHOD:

Combine all ingredients in crock pot except margarine and cheese.
Dot with margarine and sprinkle with cheese.
Cook 1-1/2 hours or until vegetables are tender.

SERVES:6

FAT GRAMS PER SERVING: FAT FREE

Nutritional Analysis Per Serving:

cal	*g. fat*	*(%of cal)*	*g.fib*	*mg.chol*	*mg. sod*
67	*0 .49*	*7*	*2.38*	*0.00*	*373*

DESSERTS

INDEX TO DESSERTS

7-UP CAKE

1 box lemon cake mix
1 box lemon pudding mix
3/4 cup applesauce
8 ounces fat free egg substitute
1 10-ounce bottle Diet 7-Up
1 small can crushed pineapples

METHOD:

Mix all ingredients and pour into a sprayed and floured 9x13 inch pan. Bake at 350 degrees until done.
Top with crushed pineapple.

SERVES: 12

FAT GRAMS PER SERVING: 4

Nutritional Analysis Per Serving:

cal	*g. fat*	*(% of cal)*	*g.fib*	*mg. chol*	*mg. sod*
243	*3.57*	*13*	*0.49*	*0.00*	*371*

ANGEL DESSERT

1 angel food cake from the bakery
2 1.34 ounces Sugar Free vanilla instant pudding
4 cups skim milk
2 1/2-pt containers Fat free sour cream
1 can blueberry pie filling

METHOD:

Break angel food cake into pieces and line bottom of 8x12-inch pan.
Prepare pudding according to instruction.
After pudding has set add sour cream to pudding.
Pour over angel food cake.
Top with layer of blueberry pie filling.

SERVES: 12

FAT GRAMS PER SERVING: FAT FREE

Nutritional Analysis Per Serving:

cal	*g. fat*	*(%of cal)*	*g.fib*	*mg.chol*	*mg. sod*
321	*0.30*	*1*	*1.87*	*4*	*619*

BAKED CUSTARD

8 ounces fat free egg substitute
1/2 cup sugar
4 cups skim milk, scalded
1 teaspoon vanilla
1/4 teaspoon salt

METHOD:

Beat together slightly the egg substitute, sugar, milk, salt and vanilla.
Put in glass baking dish and set dish in a pan with 1 inch of water.
Bake at 350 degrees for 60 minutes.

SERVES:8

FAT GRAMS PER SERVING: FAT FREE

Nutritional Analysis Per Serving:

cal	*g. fat*	*(% of cal)*	*g.fib*	*mg. chol*	*mg. sod*
110	*0.20*	*2*	*0.00*	*2*	*249*

Can't Do Anymore?

Do you feel like the load is too heavy? Do you find yourself saying, "I can't do anymore."

Maybe the wrong person is carrying most of the load. Jesus said, "My yoke is easy, and My load is light."

We are yoked up with Jesus like a pair of oxen. The pair works best when they work and stay together. If one tries to get ahead, it makes the work harder.

Jesus also said that His load is light. If the load is too heavy, maybe it isn't from Jesus. Maybe it is something you want to do. God isn't in any hurry.

Work together as a team. In the Parable of the Talents, the Good Book says that the master gave to each one according to his own ability.

It would seem that God won't give you more than you can handle, or He will give you what you need to do the job.

Take a look and see if you are equally yoked and who the load (work) belongs to.

BANANA PUDDING

3/4 cup granulated sugar
3 tablespoons all-purpose flour
Dash of salt
8 ounces fat free egg substitute
2 cups skim milk
1/2 teaspoon vanilla extract
27 low fat graham crackers
5-6 bananas
3 egg whites
2 tablespoons sugar

METHOD:

Combine 3/4 cup sugar, salt and flour in top of double boiler.
Mix in egg substitute; stir in milk and cook, uncovered, over boiling water, stirring constantly, until thickened.
Remove from heat and stir in vanilla.
In a 1 1/2-quart casserole dish layer graham crackers, bananas (sliced) and pudding mixture until you use all of mixture.
Beat 3 egg whites stiff, adding 2 tablespoons sugar, and beat until mixture forms peaks.
Pile on top of pudding.
Bake in preheated oven (425 degrees) until golden brown, or omit the whites and cover with lite cool whip.

SERVES: 6

FAT GRAMS PER SERVING: 2

Note: Nutri. Analysis includes Meringue

Nutritional Analysis Per Serving:

cal	*g. fat*	*(% of cal)*	*g.fib*	*mg. chol*	*mg. sod*
355	*1.65*	*4*	*4.26*	*1*	*392*

BLUEBERRY MERINGUE PIE

1 1/4 low fat graham cracker crumbs
2 tablespoons sugar
3/4 cup sugar
1/4 teaspoon salt
1 1/2 cups fresh blueberries
1/4 cup soft fat free margarine
4 egg whites
1/2 teaspoon almond flavoring
1/2 teaspoon cream of tartar

METHOD:

Mix crumbs, margarine and 2 tablespoons sugar in bowl.
Press mixture into bottom and sides of an ungreased 9-inch pie plate.
Bake shell in 375 degree oven for 10 minutes.
Cool.
Beat egg whites until soft peaks form.
Gradually add 3/4 cup sugar in very small amounts, beating continuously after each addition.
Alternately add almond extract, salt and cream of tartar. Carefully fold in blueberries.
Pile into baked crumb crust.
Bake in 300 degree oven for about 15 minutes or just until top browns slightly.

SERVES: 6

FAT GRAMS PER SERVING: 1

Nutritional Analysis Per Serving:

cal	*g. fat*	*(%of cal)*	*g.fib*	*mg.chol*	*mg. sod*
190	*0.90*	*4*	*0.98*	*0.00*	*318*

BUTTER CAKE

1 package Light yellow cake mix
4 ounces fat free egg substitute
4 ounces fat free margarine, melted
8 ounce package fat free cream cheese
1 box powdered sugar (save small amount to sprinkle on top)

METHOD:

Mix cake mix, egg substitute and margarine.
Press into 9x13-inch pan, which has been sprayed and floured.
Mix cream cheese with powdered sugar.
Spread on cake mixture.
Bake at 325 degrees for 40 minutes.
When cool, sprinkle with powdered sugar.
Serve cold.

SERVES: 12

FAT GRAMS PER SERVING: 2

Nutritional Analysis Per Serving:

cal	*g. fat*	*(% of cal)*	*g.fib*	*mg. chol*	*mg. sod*
371	*2.08*	*5*	*0.49*	*3*	*541*

BROKEN GLASS SQUARES

1/4 cup fat free margarine
1 1/4 cups low fat graham cracker (about 35 crackers)
1/4 cup sugar
4 1/2 cups hot tap water
1 3-ounce package strawberry or raspberry flavored Jello
1 (3 ounce) package lime flavored Jello
1 cup orange juice
1/4 cup sugar
1 (3 ounce) package lemon flavored Jello
2 cups Light whipped topping.

METHOD:

Place margarine in 2-quart utility dish.
Heat on full power for 45 seconds to 1 minute 15 seconds, or until melted. Blend in crumbs and 1/4 cup sugar.
Press mixture firmly against bottom of dish. Cook on full power for 1 to 2 1/2 minutes, or until set. Turn half-turn halfway through cooking time. Place water in 2-quart glass dish.
Heat on full power for 7 1/2 to 9 1/2 minutes, or until boiling. Place orange, strawberry and lime flavored Jello in separate 9x5x2-inch loaf pans or dishes. Pour 1 1/2 cups boiling water over each flavor Jello. Stir until dissolved. Chill until set. Cut into 1/2 inch cubes.
Place orange juice in 2 cup glass dish. Heat on Full Power for 2 to 3 minutes or until boiling.
Combine 1/4 cup sugar and lemon flavored Jello in large mixing bowl. Pour boiling orange juice over Jello mixture stirring until dissolved. Let cool, until the consistency of egg white. Fold in whipped topping. Carefully stir in Jello cubes. Pour mixture over crust. Chill for 4 to 6 hours.

SERVES: 12

FAT GRAMS PER SERVING: 2

Nutritional Analysis Per Serving:

cal	*g. fat*	*(%of cal)*	*g.fib*	*mg.chol*	*mg. sod*
115	*1.77*	*14*	*0.04*	*0.00*	*160*

Air Condition?

I heard a story about a native in Africa who went to several church meetings. I am not sure of the truth of the story but I am sure about the message it tells. During each meeting, as the crowds would come into the buildings, it would start to get very hot. The man noticed that whenever it got hot, the minister went over to the wall, turned a knob, and in minutes it would get cool. This went on for several days. Then the man went to the store and bought one of those knobs. He took it home. Put it on his wall. Turned the knob. And he waited. It never got cool. He went back to the minister to ask about it. The minister then showed him how the knob was connected to an air-conditioning unit. Our life as Christians are hopefully something for others to see, but we also need to show them the source of our strength.

CHERRY DELITE

2 angel food cakes
1 1/2 cup powdered sugar
12 ounces fat free cream cheese
2 8 ounce containers of Lite Cool Whip
1 10 ounce can Lite cherry pie filling

METHOD:

Break cake into bite-size pieces.
Set aside.
Mix powdered sugar and cream cheese until well blended.
Add Cool Whip, mix well.
Cover bottom of 9x13 pan with pieces of cake.
Spread mixture on top; continue to alternate.
Top with cherries.
Let set 3 to 4 hours.

SERVES: 12

FAT GRAMS PER SERVING:3

Nutritional Analysis Per Serving:

cal	*g. fat*	*(%of cal)*	*g.fib*	*mg.chol*	*mg. sod*
444	*2.71*	*5*	*1.34*	*4*	*686*

CHERRY CAKE

1 package Light white cake mix
8 ounces lite cool whip
1 can Light cherry pie filling

METHOD:

Bake and cool cake mix, following mix directions.
Use a 9x13-inch pan.
Spread top of cake with whipped topping.
Spread topping with cherry pie filling.
Refrigerate.
Serve cold.

Serves: 12

FAT GRAMS PER SERVING: 5

NOTE: N. analysis is based on cake being prepared with fat free egg substitute.

Nutritional Analysis Per Serving:

cal	*g. fat*	*(% of cal)*	*g.fib*	*mg. chol*	*mg. sod*
321	*4.86*	*14*	*1.38*	*0.00*	*159*

"I TRIED SEVERAL WAYS TO LOSE WEIGHT. THEN I FOUND NATOMA'S PROGRAM."

CARAMEL CAKE

1 3/4 cups flour
1 1/2 cups firmly packed Light brown sugar
1 1/2 teaspoon cinnamon
1/2 teaspoon salt
1/2 teaspoon baking soda
1/2 teaspoon baking powder
1 teaspoon vanilla extract
3/4 cup fat free margarine, softened
6 ounces fat free egg substitute
1 1/2 cups peeled and diced apples
1 cup Grape Nuts cereal
1 cup raisins (if desired)

METHOD:

Preheat oven to 350 degrees, 325 degrees for glass dish.
Spray a 13x9-inch pan.
Lightly spoon flour into measuring cup and level off. In a large bowl, combine the first 9 ingredients and beat 3 minutes at medium speed.
Stir in apples, nuts and raisins.
Pour into a sprayed pan.
Bake 30 to 40 minutes, until toothpick comes out clean.
Let cool. If using self-rising flour, omit the salt, baking powder and baking soda.

CARAMEL CAKE CON'D

FROSTING:

1 1/2 cups powdered sugar
1/4 teaspoon cinnamon
1/4 cup fat free margarine, softened
1/2 teaspoon vanilla extract
3-4 tablespoons skim milk

METHOD:

Blend until smooth; spread over cake.

SERVES: 12

FAT GRAMS PER SERVING: FAT FREE

Nutritional Analysis Per Serving:

cal	*g. fat*	*(%of cal)*	*g.fib*	*mg.chol*	*mg. sod*
250	*0.38*	*1*	*1.05*	*0.00*	*278*

CHOCOLATE BUNDT CAKE

1 package Chocolate Dream cake mix
1 large package Sugar Free instant chocolate pudding
8 ounces fat free sour cream
1/2 cup applesauce
1/2 cup warm water
8 ounces fat free egg substitute
6 ounces chocolate chips

METHOD:

Mix well with electric mixer.
Add 1 small (6 ounce) package chocolate chips.
Bake at 375 degrees for 55 minutes in a sprayed and floured Bundt pan.
Leave in the pan for 20 minutes after baking, then turn out of the pan.

SERVES: 12

FAT GRAMS PER SERVING: 11

Nutritional Analysis Per Serving:

cal	*g. fat*	*(% of cal)*	*g.fib*	*mg. chol*	*mg. sod*
303	*10.92*	*32*	*0.65*	*1*	*560*

Fall

Fall is such a beautiful time of the year in the north, when the different leaves starts to turn all the varieties of colors.

Some people drive for hours just to see the landscape painted by God.

After the death of a loved one, God showed me that the beauty in fall happens as the trees prepare for the winter, and the leaves start to die.

God showed me that there can be beauty in death when we look at it from His point of view.

God's Word says that to be absent from the body is to be present with Him if you are one of His children.

It is like in some parts of the south where they have a sad funeral procession to the grave site because of the loss, but then celebrate afterwards. God says,

"All things work together for good to those that love Him." (Romans 8:28) God also gives His Holy Spirit as a comforter.

CLASSIC PUMPKIN PIE

4 ounce fat free egg substitute, slightly beaten
3/4 cup light brown sugar, packed
1 to 1 1/2 teaspoon cinnamon
1/4 teaspoon cloves
1 2/3 cup evaporated skim milk
Unbaked pastry shell
1 16-ounce can pumpkin
1 teaspoon salt
1/2 teaspoon ginger
Dash nutmeg
1/2 teaspoon vanilla

METHOD:

Combine all ingredients and pour into pastry shell.
Bake at 425 degrees for 15 minutes, reduce temperature to 350 degrees and bake 40 to 45 minutes longer, or until knife inserted in center comes out clean.
Garnish with lite cool whip.

SERVES: 8

FAT GRAMS PER SERVING: 11

NOTE: N. analysis does NOT include whip topping.

Nutritional Analysis Per Serving:

cal	*g. fat*	*(% of cal)*	*g.fib*	*mg. chol*	*mg. sod*
274	*10.71*	*35*	*4.19*	*5*	*359*

COBBLER SURPRISE

1 cup sugar
1 cup flour
3/4 cup skim milk
2 teaspoons baking powder
1/2 teaspoon salt
1/2 cup fat free margarine
16 ounce can peaches

METHOD:

Make batter with sugar, flour, milk, baking powder and salt.
Preheat oven to 350 degrees.
Melt margarine in large casserole dish (hot).
Pour batter evenly over hot margarine.
Spoon fruit over batter.
Bake at 350 degrees for 30 to 45 minutes until brown on top.

SERVES: 6

FAT GRAMS PER SERVING: FAT FREE

Nutritional Analysis Per Serving:

cal	*g. fat*	*(%of cal)*	*g.fib*	*mg.chol*	*mg. sod*
167	*0.28*	*1*	*0.89*	*1*	*346*

BOILED ICING

1 1/2 cups sugar, divided
3/4 cup water
1 tablespoon light corn syrup
2 egg whites
1/8 teaspoon salt
1 teaspoon vanilla

METHOD:

Reserve 2 tablespoons of the sugar.
Combine remaining sugar with water and corn syrup in a heavy saucepan.
Cook over medium heat stirring constantly until sugar dissolves and syrup is clear.
Cook without stirring to soft ball stage (240 degrees).
Remove from heat.
Quickly beat egg whites and salt until soft peaks form, gradually adding reserved sugar.
Beat until blended.
Continue to beat, slowly adding syrup mix. Add vanilla and beat until stiff peaks form and frosting is thick.

YIELDS: 4 cups frosting

FAT GRAMS PER SERVING: FAT FREE

Nutritional Analysis Per Serving:

cal	*g. fat*	*(% of cal)*	*g.fib*	*mg. chol*	*mg. sod*
48	*0*	*0*	*0*	*0.00*	*23*

Rejection???

Most people do not handle rejection with the greatest of ease.

The bigger the rejection, the harder it is to deal with and try to get over. Some people carry scars of rejection with them most of their lives.

The hurt and pain of rejection is probably the hardest thing in life to overcome. Some people withdraw within themselves and others are always trying to get even, but nothing they do is ever enough.

Jesus suffered great rejection at His trial and on the cross. His closest friends turned their backs on Him and even denied knowing Him.

COFFEE CAKE

1 1/2 cups sifted flour
1/2 cup sugar
2 teaspoons baking powder
1/2 teaspoon salt
4 ounces fat free egg substitute
1/4 cup applesauce
1/2 cup pineapple juice
1/3 cup Grape Nuts cereal
1 cup pineapple chunks

METHOD:

Sift together the dry ingredients.
Beat fat free egg substitute; combine liquid and dry ingredients and beat until smooth.
Spread in long baking dish.
On top of cake mixture, put pieces of well-drained pineapple chunks.
Sprinkle Grape Nuts on top, then sprinkle crumbs made of the following:
2/3 cup sugar
2/3 cup flour
6 tablespoons fat free margarine
Cinnamon to taste

METHOD:

Blend sugar, flour and margarine well with fingers until crumbs. Bake at 350 degrees for 45 minutes to 1 hour or until done.

SERVES: 8

FAT GRAMS PER SERVING: FAT FREE

Nutritional Analysis Per Serving:

cal	*g. fat*	*(% of cal)*	*g.fib*	*mg. chol*	*mg. sod*
255	*0.42*	*1*	*2.08*	*0.00*	*356*

COOKED CREAM FILLING

1 cup skim milk
4 ounces fat free egg substitute
6 tablespoons sugar
4 tablespoons flour
Few grains salt
1/2 teaspoon vanilla

METHOD:

Scald the milk in the top of a double boiler.
Beat the fat free egg substitute in a bowl; add the sugar, flour and salt. Slowly stir the hot milk into this.
Return to the double boiler and cook until the mixture thickens, stirring frequently.
When cool, add the vanilla.

SERVES: 2

FAT GRAMS PER SERVING: FAT FREE

Nutritional Analysis Per Serving:

cal	*g. fat*	*(%of cal)*	*g.fib*	*mg.chol*	*mg. sod*
248	*0.35*	*1*	*0.42*	*2*	*387*

COTTAGE CHEESE PIE

CRUST:

3 cup fine low fat graham cracker crumbs
1/2 cup sugar (or less)
1/2 cup melted fat free margarine

METHOD:

Combine and pat into pie pan, reserving 1/2 cup of the crumb mixture for topping.
Filling:
1 pound fat free cottage cheese
1/3 cup sugar
1/2 teaspoon salt
1/2 cup skim milk
12 ounces fat free egg substitute
2 tablespoons melted fat free margarine
2 1/2 teaspoon juice and rind of 1 lemon

METHOD:

Set the oven to 350 degrees.
Process the cottage cheese, then add sugar, salt, milk, egg substitute, melted margarine and lemon juice and rind.
Pour into prepared pie shell and sprinkle remaining crumbs over the top.
Bake 1 hour.
SERVES:8

FAT GRAMS PER SERVING: 1

Nutritional Analysis Per Serving:

cal	*g. fat*	*(% of cal)*	*g.fib*	*mg. chol*	*mg. sod*
352	*1.41*	*4*	*0.10*	*5*	*1011*

CREAMY TOPPED CHOCOLATE PIE

1 low fat 9-inch graham cracker pie crust, cooked and cooled
3 1/2 cups cold skim milk
2 (4-serving size) packages sugar free Jell-O chocolate flavor instant pudding and pie filling

CREAM CHEESE TOPPING:

1 (3 ounce) package fat free cream cheese, softened
1 tablespoon sugar
3 tablespoons skim milk
2 cups lite cool whip

METHOD:

Prepare pie filling on package, using 3 1/2 cups milk.
Pour into pie shell.
Refrigerate for at least 1 hour.
Beat cheese with sugar and milk in a bowl until well blended and smooth.
Fold in whipped topping.
Spread over pie before serving.

SERVES:8

FAT GRAMS PER SERVING: 2

Nutritional Analysis Per Serving:

cal	*g. fat*	*(%of cal)*	*g.fib*	*mg.chol*	*mg. sod*
126	*2.18*	*16*	*1*	*3*	*439*

A Father's Love

A father's and a mother's love of their children seems to be so one-sided until their children have children of their own.

All of the sleepless nights when they needed feeding, got sick, got their first teeth, needed a diaper changed or any other number of reasons you never thought could happen.

Trips to the doctor, hospital, day-care, school, special activities and trips of "just because." The concerns for and expense of food, clothing, shelter and the other things already mentioned may mean both parents have to work and even need a part-time job. When children become a teenager, they may feel like no one even loves them.

For some reason they forget the early years of sacrifices made on their behalf. To the parents, it seems like it was all a one-sided love. Then the children have children of their own and all of a sudden, a new appreciation develops for what their parents went through.

God has done a lot for us as His children. His love covered everything we needed. Sometimes it takes us a long time to appreciate all of our heavenly Father's love.

"SOMETIMES I FEEL LIKE I'M WAY IN OVER MY HEAD WITH THIS WEIGHT LOSS BUSINESS."

CRANBERRY LEMON COFFEE CAKE

1/4 cup applesauce
1 cup sugar
4 ounces fat free egg substitute
2 cups sifted all-purpose flour
2 teaspoons baking powder
3/4 cup skim milk
1 teaspoon lemon extract
1/2 cup grape nuts

METHOD:

Cream applesauce and sugar until light and fluffy.
Beat fat free egg substitute and add to creamed mixture.
Mix and sift the dry ingredients and add alternately with the milk to the first mixture. Add flavoring.
Pour into sprayed 8x8x2-inch pan, and spread the following topping evenly and lightly over the top of the batter.

CRANBERRY LEMON CONT'D

CRANBERRY TOPPING:

3 tablespoons sugar
1 teaspoon grated lemon rind
1/4 teaspoon cinnamon
Dash nutmeg
2/3 cup Ocean Spray Jellied Cranberry Sauce, diced

METHOD:

Mix sugar and lemon rind well.
Add spices and 1/2 cup Grape Nuts.
Add cranberry sauce last, just before spreading.
Bake in a moderate oven, 350 degrees, for 50 minutes or until cake is done.

SERVES: 6

FAT GRAMS PER SERVING: 1

Nutritional Analysis Per Serving:

cal	*g. fat*	*(%of cal)*	*g.fib*	*mg.chol*	*mg. sod*
363	*0.60*	*1*	*3.05*	*0.50*	*379*

CREAM CHEESE TOPPING:

1 (3 ounce) package fat free cream cheese, softened
1 tablespoon sugar
3 tablespoons skim milk
2 cups lite cool whip

METHOD:

Prepare pie filling on package, using 3 1/2 cups milk.
Pour into pie shell.
Refrigerate for at least 1 hour.
Meanwhile, prepare topping.
Beat cheese with sugar and milk in a bowl until well blended and smooth.
Fold in whipped topping.
Spread over pie before serving.

SERVES: 6

FAT GRAMS PER SERVING: 1

Nutritional Analysis Per Serving:

cal	*g. fat*	*(% of cal)*	*g.fib*	*mg. chol*	*mg. sod*
363	*0.60*	*1*	*3.05*	*0.50*	*379*

LEMON PUDDING CAKE

8 ounces fat free egg substitute
2/3 cup lemon juice
1 teaspoon lemon rind
1 tablespoon melted fat free margarine
1 1/2 cups sugar
1/2 cup flour
1/2 teaspoon salt
1/2 cup skim milk

METHOD:

Beat the first 4 ingredients all together until thick and lemon colored.
Combine the next 3 ingredients all together and add to the egg mixture with, milk, alternately, beating well.
Blend into batter, using low speed on mixer.
Pour into 8-inch square baking dish.
Set in pan of hot water.
Bake at 350 degrees for 45 minutes.

SERVES: 8

FAT GRAMS PER SERVING: FAT FREE

Nutritional Analysis Per Serving:

cal	*g. fat*	*(%of cal)*	*g.fib*	*mg.chol*	*mg. sod*
96	*0.13*	*1*	*0.25*	*0.25*	*108*

Couch Potato?

TV has created many new ways of life and new meanings to many words.

The cartoons and jokes about "couch potatoes" draw up pictures in our minds of someone who has become very lazy and overweight.

Today, in America, we could say many Christians have become used to pastors or teachers doing the studying for us.

We just want to listen. Then we become very fat on all the Word that we have heard and get too lazy to do anything.

God didn't call us to be pew potatoes, but He said to **go out.**

God isn't going to look at how many times we were in the pew, but how many times we got out of the pews to do what we have heard. The Good Book, the Word is said to be "living and active."

The Word in us should make us living and active. Don't get too comfortable.

God has a way of getting us moving.

LOW FAT GRAHAM CRACKER, CRUST, FAT FREE (9 INCH)

1 1/2 cups crushed low fat graham crackers
1/4 cup famous brand FAT FREE margarine
3 tablespoons sugar

METHOD:

Crush enough crackers to measure 1 1/2 cups.
Stir in the margarine. Add sugar.
Mix well and press into bottom and up sides of a 9-inch pie plate.
Bake about 10 minutes in 400-degree oven.

SERVES: 1

FATS PER SERVING: 3

WATCH THOSE CALORIES!

Nutritional Analysis Per Serving:

cal	g. fat	(%of cal)	g.fib	mg.chol	mg. sod
340	3.33	9	2.22	0.00	942

MEATS

INDEX TO MEATS

A-1 MEAT LOAF

1 pound ground turkey breast
1/2 cup fat free dry bread crumbs
1/3 cup finely minced onions
1/2 cup chopped green peppers
1 8-ounce can tomato sauce
3 tablespoons A-1 sauce
1 ounce fat free egg substitute
1 teaspoon garlic powder
3/4 teaspoon oregano
3/4 teaspoon basil
1/4 cup shredded fat free Mozzarella cheese

METHOD:

Combine all ingredients except cheese.
Lightly pack in 9x5-inch loaf pan.
Bake at 350 degrees for 50 minutes.
Drain.
Top with cheese.
Bake 5 minutes until cheese melts.

SERVES: 6

FAT GRAMS PER SERVING: FAT FREE

Nutritional Analysis Per Serving:

cal	*g. fat*	*(% of cal)*	*g.fib*	*mg. chol*	*mg. sod*
96	*0.26*	*2*	*2.24*	*9*	*674*

BAKED CHICKEN

8 boneless skinless chicken breasts
2 teaspoons salt
6 tablespoons fat free margarine
2 1/2 cups water
2/3 cup flour
1/4 teaspoon pepper
1 medium onion, chopped

METHOD:

Combine 1/3 cup flour, 1 1/2 teaspoon salt and 1/4 teaspoon pepper in bag.
Shake chicken pieces to coat evenly.
Brown pieces, part at a time, in margarine in nonstick skillet. Place in single layer in large roasting pan.
Saute onion until soft in drippings and stir in 1 1/2 cups water and remaining 1/2 teaspoon salt.
Heat, stirring constantly, to boiling.
Pour over chicken and cover.
Bake in 350 degree oven for one hour or until chicken is tender.
Remove to platter and make gravy by blending 1/3 cup flour and 1 cup water until smooth.
Slowly stir flour mixture into liquid in pan.
Cook, stirring constantly, until gravy thickens.

SERVES: 8

FAT GRAMS PER SERVING: 3

Nutritional Analysis Per Serving:

cal	*g. fat*	*(%of cal)*	*g.fib*	*mg.chol*	*mg. sod*
179	*3.13*	*16*	*0.75*	*67*	*397*

"*WE DONT COUNT CALORIES. AND WE DON'T WANT PEOPLE TO GET HOOKED ON SCALES.*"

BARBECUED CHICKEN

1 large onion
2 teaspoons salt
6 boneless skinless chicken breasts
3/4 cup chopped celery
2 tablespoons Worcestershire sauce
1/2 cup flour
1/4 teaspoon pepper
1 cup catsup
1 tablespoon brown sugar

METHOD:

Peel and slice onion and separate into rings.
Wash and pat chicken dry.
Dip chicken in mixture of flour, salt and pepper.
Brown coated chicken in Nonstick skillet.
Remove chicken to baking dish.
Add onion rings and saute in fat free margarine until golden.
Stir in celery, catsup, water, Worcestershire and brown sugar.
Simmer five minutes and pour over browned chicken.
Cover and bake in 350 degree oven for one hour or until chicken is done.

SERVES: 6

FAT GRAMS PER SERVING: 4

Nutritional Analysis Per Serving:

cal	*g. fat*	*(%of cal)*	*g.fib*	*mg.chol*	*mg. sod*
308	*3.59*	*11*	*2.62*	*67*	*1896*

BREAKFAST SAUSAGE & GRAVY

1 pound turkey sausage
3 tablespoons fat free margarine
2 tablespoons flour
1 1/2 cup evaporated skim milk

METHOD:

Pat out 6 3-ounce sausage patties.
Cook in iron skillet until done.
Remove patties from skillet.
Drain excess grease.
There will be a substance left in the skillet.
Melt margarine in skillet; stir until brown.
Add flour and stir until mixed well.
Gradually add milk until desired thickness.
Salt and pepper to taste.

SERVES: 4

FAT GRAMS PER SERVING: 10

EXCELLENT WITH LOW FAT CAN BISCUITS.

3 BISCUITS = 2 FAT GRAMS

Nutritional Analysis Per Serving:

cal	*g. fat*	*(% of cal)*	*g.fib*	*mg. chol*	*mg. sod*
236	*9.83*	*37*	*0.10*	*69*	*694*

BURRITOS

1 1-pound pkg. pinto beans
1 teaspoon cumin
2 tablespoons chili powder
1/4 teaspoon garlic to taste
2 teaspoon pepper

METHOD:

Wash beans and drain, in fresh water.
Boil beans until tender, then drain and mash beans in mixer.
Then add seasonings and a little juice until creamy.

MEAT:

2 1/2 pounds ground turkey breast
1 to 2 chopped onions
2 bell peppers, chopped
1 clove garlic, finely chopped
2 teaspoons cumin
2 tablespoons chili powder, garlic powder, salt and pepper

METHOD:

Brown meat, onions, bell pepper and garlic until meat changes color and onions are transparent.
Add seasonings and cook about 30 minutes, adding a little water.
When meat tastes done, add bean mixture to the meat, stirring well.
Heat fat free tortillas in sprayed Nonstick skillet and roll.
You can heat tortillas in microwave oven, but only a few seconds as they get hard, and you cannot roll them.
Also you can freeze these burritos and use as needed.

SERVES: 6

FAT GRAMS PER SERVING: 1

Nutritional Analysis Per Serving:

cal	*g. fat*	*(%of cal)*	*g.fib*	*mg.chol*	*mg. sod*
302	*1.04*	*3*	*7.54*	*13*	*440*

CHEESE SAUCE FOR SPAGHETTI

6 boneless, skinless chicken breasts
1 cups of a block fat free cheese
2 cups or more fat free chicken broth
1/2 cup chopped onions
1 rib celery
1 small bell pepper
3/4 pound tomatoes
1 can cream of chicken soup
2 teaspoons chili powder
garlic powder, and pepper to taste

METHOD:

Add chopped onions, celery and bell pepper to broth; let simmer about 20 minutes.
Then add cheese and let melt.
Add chopped tomatoes
Let this simmer about 20 minutes.
Add seasonings (pepper, chili powder and garlic).
Add meat last, cook on low until chicken is done.

SERVES: 8

FAT GRAMS PER SERVING: 5

Nutritional Analysis Per Serving:

cal	*g. fat*	*(% of cal)*	*g.fib*	*mg. chol*	*mg. sod*
235	*4.74*	*18*	*1.25*	*62*	*1365*

CHICKEN DELUXE

6 boneless skinless chicken breasts
1/2 10 3/4-ounce can cream of chicken soup
1/2 10 3/4-ounce can cream of celery soup
1/2 cup water
3/4 cup fat free cheddar cheese, shredded
3 green onions, sliced

METHOD:

Arrange chicken in sprayed 2-quart baking dish.
Combine soups and water.
Stir in shredded cheese and finely sliced onions.
Pour over breasts and bake uncovered in 300 degree oven for 1 1/2 hours or until done.

SERVES: 6

FAT GRAMS PER SERVING: 6

Nutritional Analysis Per Serving:

cal	*g. fat*	*(%of cal)*	*g.fib*	*mg.chol*	*mg. sod*
197	*5.65*	*26*	*0.42*	*74*	*640*

CHICKEN OR TURKEY TETRAZZINI

6 boneless, skinless chicken breasts
1 onion, chopped
1/2 bell pepper
2 ribs celery
3 tablespoons fat free margarine
1/2 can cream of celery soup
1/2 can cream of mushroom soup
1 8 ounce package spaghetti
1 cup grated fat free Cheddar cheese
1 1/2 cups skim milk

METHOD:

Wash chicken.
Boil and shred chicken.
Saute onions, bell pepper, celery and margarine.
Boil and rinse spaghetti.
Add rest of ingredients, using only half of cheese.
Put in pan and top with remaining cheese.
Bake at 350 degrees until bubbly.

SERVES: 8

FAT GRAMS PER SERVING: 5

Nutritional Analysis Per Serving:

cal	*g. fat*	*(% of cal)*	*g.fib*	*mg. chol*	*mg. sod*
288	*5.13*	*16*	*1.54*	*56*	*581*

Snacks

I love snacks. Pretzels and popcorn are my two favorites.

Snacks aren't a meal. They are something I like, that holds me over till I eat another meal or go to bed.

When I eat a snack, I find that I don't generally overeat at mealtime. (I know that we aren't all the same.) If I overeat, I get lazy.

Daily Living are like snacks. They aren't meant to be a whole meal. Just something that you will hopefully like, and hold you over till your next full meal.

They aren't fatty snacks, but they do contain lots of God's food and seeds. Make some of your own. Take Daily Living.

See how The Good Book is evident and practical to everything in life.

His Word is not just good reading, but a guide for everyday living.

Sixty-six books, all in one, with all the wisdom, knowledge and understanding you could ever need.

CHICKEN PARMESAN

8 boneless, skinless chicken breasts
2 cups fat free bread crumbs
1/4 cup minced parsley
1/4 teaspoon pepper to taste
2 cups fat free margarine, melted
3/4 cups grated fat free Parmesan
3/4 cup sharp cheese
Garlic salt as desired

METHOD:

Wash and pat chicken dry.
Combine all dry ingredients.
Dip each chicken breast in melted margarine.
Shake in bag with crumb mixture.
Place in shallow baking pan.
Pour over them any remaining margarine, if needed, to avoid chicken drying out in pan.
Bake 1 1/2 hours in 325 degree oven or until meat is done.

SERVES: 8

FAT GRAMS PER SERVING: 3

Nutritional Analysis Per Serving:

cal	*g. fat*	*(% of cal)*	*g.fib*	*mg. chol*	*mg. sod*
274	*3.01*	*10*	*2.57*	*69*	*881*

ITALIAN CHICKEN (CROCKPOT)

6 boneless, skinless chicken breasts, cut up
2 medium onions, thinly sliced
2 cloves garlic, minced
1 pound fresh tomatoes
1 8-ounce can tomato sauce
1/2 cup diced green pepper
1 teaspoon oregano
1/2 teaspoon basil
1/2 teaspoon celery seed
1/4 teaspoon pepper
1/4 teaspoon cayenne
1 bay leaf, crumbled
1/4 cup water

METHOD:

Wash and pat chicken dry.
Cook chicken pieces in Nonstick skillet.
Place chicken in crockpot, cover with onion slices, then add all other ingredients.
Cook on low 6-8 hours, or on high 3-4 hours.

SERVES: 6

FAT GRAMS PER SERVING: 4

Nutritional Analysis Per Serving:

cal	*g. fat*	*(%of cal)*	*g.fib*	*mg.chol*	*mg. sod*
270	*3.88*	*13*	*5.72*	*67*	*849*

CLASSIC MEAT LOAF (MICROWAVE)

SAUCE:

1/3 cup catsup
1 teaspoon Worcestershire sauce
1 tablespoon Lite dark brown sugar
1 tablespoon prepared mustard

MEAT LOAF:

1 1/2 pounds lean ground beef
1 8-ounce can tomato sauce
4 ounces fat free egg substitute
1/2 cup fat free bread crumbs
1 tablespoon instant minced onion
1/4 tablespoon instant minced garlic
1/4 teaspoon pepper

CLASSIC MEATLOAF CONT'D

METHOD:

Combine all sauce ingredients in small bowl.
Set aside.
Combine all ingredients for meat loaf in large bowl.
Mix well.
Pat into 9x5x2-inch loaf dish.
Cook on full power for 6 minutes.
Pour sauce over meat loaf.
Continue cooking on Cook Level 3 for 25 to 30 minutes, or until temperature of 160 degrees F is reached.
For a firmer meat loaf, decrease tomato sauce to 3/4 cup.
If desired, add remaining tomato sauce to meat loaf sauce.
Use temperature probe to heat to 160 degrees F, if your microwave oven has this feature.

Serves: 8

FAT GRAMS PER SERVING: 4

Nutritional Analysis Per Serving:

cal	*g. fat*	*(%of cal)*	*g.fib*	*mg.chol*	*mg. sod*
169	*3.54*	*19*	*1.83*	*30*	*826*

JALAPENO PIE

4 chopped jalapeno peppers
16 ounces fat free Cheddar cheese
1 pound ground turkey breast
2 8-ounce cartons fat free egg substitute

METHOD:

In a 9x13-inch size pan layer jalapeno peppers on bottom of greased pan.
Next layer grated Cheddar.
Then later brown seasoned ground turkey.
Drain, mix with egg substitute.
Pour over peppers.
Bake at 350 degrees for 45 minutes.

SERVES: 6

FAT GRAMS PER SERVING: FAT FREE

Nutritional Analysis Per Serving:

cal	*g. fat*	*(% of cal)*	*g.fib*	*mg. chol*	*mg. sod*
627	*0.17*	*<1%*	*0.41*	*51*	*2949*

LASAGNA

1/2 pound lean ground sirloin
1 1/2 tablespoons garlic powder
1 tablespoon parsley
1 tablespoon sweet basil
2 cups fresh tomatoes
2 16-ounce cans tomato paste
10 ounces lasagna noodles
3 cups fat free cottage cheese
1/2 cup fat free egg substitute (equal to 2 eggs)
1/2 teaspoon pepper
2 tablespoons parsley
1/4 cup fat free Parmesan cheese
1/2 pound fat free shredded mozzarella cheese

METHOD:

Brown and drain meat.
Add next 6 ingredients, simmer uncovered 30 minutes, stirring occasionally.
Cook noodles in water, drain and rinse.
Mix cottage cheese, egg substitute, seasonings and Parmesan cheese.
Layer noodles, 1/2 the mozzarella cheese and 1/2 the meat mixture.
Repeat layers, topping with the mozarella cheese.
Bake for 30 minutes at 375 degrees.

SERVES: 8

FAT GRAMS PER SERVING: 5

Nutritional Analysis Per Serving:

cal	*g. fat*	*(%of cal)*	*g.fib*	*mg.chol*	*mg. sod*
640	*5*	*7*	*11.54*	*65*	*1764*

LEMON CHICKEN

4 boneless skinless chicken breasts
1/4 cup fat free margarine
1/2 Garlic powder
1/2 teaspoon pepper
1/4 cup juice of one lemon
1 teaspoon Worcestershire sauce
1 tablespoon molasses
1 cup Lite dry pancake mix
1/2 teaspoon celery seed
1 tablespoon parsley
2 cups orange juice
1/4 cup Lite brown sugar

METHOD:

Wash and pat chicken dry
Roll chicken breasts in pancake mix.
Melt margarine in casserole dish and dip chicken in margarine and arrange in casserole dish.
Sprinkle to taste with seasonings.
Bake in 275 degree oven for two hours oruntil meat is almost done
Combine orange juice, lemon juice, brown sugar, Worcestershire, salt and molasses.
Pour sauce over chicken and bake, uncovered, until chicken is done at 250 degrees.

SERVES: 4

FAT GRAMS PER SERVING: 5

Nutritional Analysis Per Serving:

cal	*g. fat*	*(% of cal)*	*g.fib*	*mg. chol*	*mg. sod*
372	*4.56*	*11*	*0.34*	*79*	*637*

Cookies and Ice Cream

It would be hard to eat cookies and ice cream every day and not gain weight. It could also hurt your blood sugar level, also cause problems with your teeth and who knows what else. Potatoes are good for you but as a boy, I ate so many that the doctor told me that it was the potatoes that were causing all the sties on my eyes. Our doctor was concerned about the skin color of our baby until he found out we were feeding the baby lots of sweet potatoes and carrots. What we put into our body will eventually show up and even more so when it is done in excess. The same is true for what we put into our minds. The Word tells us that we need to renew our mind with the Word of God. That is the way that we get the mind of Christ. What we put into our mind is very important. You are the one that controls all the input. Like a computer, "junk in-junk out." It is no better than what you put in it. What are you putting into your mind?

MEAT AND TATERS

6 serving slices 95% Fat free ham, cut about 1/4 inch thick
6-8 medium potatoes, thinly sliced
1 cup chopped onion
1/4 teaspoon pepper
1 cup shredded fat free Cheddar cheese
1 can cream of celery soup
1/4 teaspoon paprika

METHOD:

Alternate ingredients in slow cooker as follows: half the ham, potatoes and onions; half the pepper; half the cheese.
Repeat with second layer.
Spread soup over food so air does not reach potatoes.
Sprinkle with paprika.
Cook on low 8-9 hours, or on high 4-5 hours.

SERVES: 6

FAT GRAMS PER SERVING: 4

Nutritional Analysis Per Serving:

cal	*g. fat*	*(% of cal)*	*g.fib*	*mg. chol*	*mg. sod*
228	*3.47*	*14*	*3.21*	*26*	*804*

NO HASSLE TUNA SKILLET

2 tablespoons fat free margarine
1 small clove garlic, minced
1/2 cup bulgur wheat
1 10-ounce package frozen peas, thawed
1/2 cup chopped onion
1 cup water
1 6-1/2-ounce can tuna water packed, drained
2 tablespoons chopped parsley
2 tablespoons raisins

METHOD:

Melt margarine and saute onion, garlic and bulgur wheat until lite brown.
Add water and bring to boil.
Cover.
Reduce heat and cook over low heat for 15 minutes.
Add tuna and remaining ingredients.
Heat thoroughly, stirring occasionally.

SERVES: 4

FAT GRAMS PER SERVING: 1

Nutritional Analysis Per Serving:

cal	*g. fat*	*(%of cal)*	*g.fib*	*mg.chol*	*mg. sod*
244	*1.23*	*5*	*10.50*	*24*	*413*

OLD FASHION COWBOY STEW

1 bell pepper
1 pound ground turkey breast
1 medium-size onion, diced
3/4 teaspoon chili powder
12 ounce can tomatoes
16 ounces red kidney beans
1 pound frozen package whole corn

METHOD:

Fry meat, onion and bell pepper in sprayed Nonstick skillet until brown.
Add chili powder, tomatoes, kidney beans and corn.
Simmer stew for about 20 minutes.
Serve with fat free crackers.

SERVES: 6

FAT GRAMS PER SERVING: 2

Nutritional Analysis Per Serving:

cal	*g. fat*	*(% of cal)*	*g.fib*	*mg. chol*	*mg. sod*
346	*2.20*	*6*	*4.57*	*9*	*737*

Sugar Or. . .

There is a song that goes, "A spoonful of sugar makes the medicine go down in a most delightful way."

There is always the other way, punishment and/or pain to get someone to do something.

The first way is operating in love, while the second way gets results by fear. God wants to love us into Heaven, not scare us into Heaven.

Both ways seem to work. However, The Good Book says, "He so loved the world, that He gave His only Son." God operates out of love. Even when God corrects us, it is out of love.

Correction out of love is a whole lot different than punishment to get even or show who is boss.

People that are punished want to get even and generally can't wait for their chance to strike back. The Good Book says, "That love never fails." The Word says that fear is not from God. Fear then comes from the enemy and he will not succeed.

OVEN FRIED CHICKEN

6 boneless, skinless chicken breasts
4 ounces fat free egg substitute, well beaten with 2 table spoons water
1/2 cup grated fat free Parmesan cheese (optional)
2 cups fat free Italian style bread crumbs
1 tub (8 ounces) fat free margarine, melted
1/4 teaspoon pepper to taste
1/4 teaspoon onion powder to taste
1/4 teaspoon garlic powder to taste

METHOD:

Wash and pat dry chicken.
Mix dry ingredients.
Dip chicken into egg substitute-water mixture and roll in crumbs. Place in foil-lined pan (pizza pan works nicely) which has been coated with part of the margarine.
Dot chicken with remaining margarine.

SERVES: 6

FAT GRAMS PER SERVING: 5

Nutritional Analysis Per Serving:

cal	*g. fat*	*(% of cal)*	*g.fib*	*mg. chol*	*mg. sod*
352	*5*	*13*	*2.68*	*67*	*1571*

PIZZA MEAT LOAF

1 pound lean ground sirloin
4 ounces fat free egg substitute, slitely beaten
1/2 cup fat free bread crumbs
1 8-ounce can pizza sauce, divided
3/4 teaspoon Italian seasoning
1/2 teaspoon ground oregano
1/4 teaspoon pepper
2 cups shredded fat free mozzarella cheese, divided

METHOD:

Combine ground beef, egg substitute, bread crumbs, 1/4 cup pizza sauce, Italian seasoning, oregano and pepper in large mixing bowl.
Mix well.
Shape meat mixture into 8X10-inch dish.
Sprinkle 1 1/2 cups cheese over meat.
Bake at 350 degrees for 1 hour or until meat is done.

SERVES: 8

FAT GRAMS PER SERVING: 2

Nutritional Analysis Per Serving:

cal	*g. fat*	*(%of cal)*	*g.fib*	*mg.chol*	*mg. sod*
155	*2.06*	*12*	*0.64*	*30*	*634*

SAUSAGE BREAKFAST BAKE

2 cups package Lite pancake mix
1 1/4 cup skim milk
4 ounces egg substitute
2 tablespoons fat free margarine, melted
1 14-ounce jar spiced apple rings
1 pound Mr. Turkey polish sausage

METHOD:

Combine pancake mix, milk, eggs and margarine; beat with mixer until nearly smooth.
Pour into greased 13x9x2-inch baking dish.
Drain apple rings, reserve syrup.
Halve sausage link, lenthwise. Arrange clockwise apple rings and sausage over batter.
Bake at 350 degrees for 30 to 35 minutes.
May be served with warm apple syrup.

SERVES: 8

FAT GRAMS PER SERVING: 3

Nutritional Analysis Per Serving:

cal	*g. fat*	*(% of cal)*	*g.fib*	*mg. chol*	*mg. sod*
231	*2.91*	*11*	*0.97*	*37*	*1030*

"I LIKE FOOD, I LIKE TO EAT, I LIKE BEING THIN. WHY NOT HAVE IT ALL?"

SHRIMP CURRY

1 pound boiled , cleaned shrimp, cut into pieces if desired
1 cup chopped onions
1/2 cup sliced celery
1 cup chopped apple
1/4 teaspoon pepper
1 tablespoon curry powder
1/4 teaspoon ginger
2 10 1/2-ounce cans condensed cream of celery soup
1 cup water
1 8-ounce package elbow macaroni, cooked

METHOD:

Combine all ingredients except macaroni in slow cooker and stir.
Cook on low 6-8 hours, or on high 4 hours.
Add cooked macaroni and heat.

SERVES: 6

FAT GRAMS PER SERVING: 5

Nutritional Analysis Per Serving:

cal	*g. fat*	*(% of cal)*	*g.fib*	*mg. chol*	*mg. sod*
262	*4.79*	*16*	*2.71*	*66*	*636*

SHRIMP PELOU

1 pound shrimp, cleaned
1 large onion
1 bell pepper
1 10 1/2-ounce can onion soup
1 10 1/2-ounce can cream of chicken soup
1 10-ounce can Ro-Tel tomatoes
7 1/2 ounce can tomato sauce
1/2 teaspoon pepper to taste
2 cups washed raw rice

METHOD:

Mix all ingredients.
Place in a large Dutch oven.
Bake 1 1/2 hours at 350 degrees.
Stir twice.

SERVES: 8

FAT GRAMS PER SERVING: 3

Nutritional Analysis Per Serving:

cal	*g. fat*	*(%of cal)*	*g.fib*	*mg.chol*	*mg. sod*
284	*3.38*	*11*	*2.36*	*46*	*1196*

SOUTHERN SPICE CHICKEN

6 boneless skinless chicken breasts
1 teaspoon pepper
1 tablespoon garlic powder
1/2 cup soy sauce
1/2 teaspoon curry powder
1/2 cup fat free Italian dressing
1 tablespoon Lite brown sugar

METHOD:

Wash and pat dry chicken.
Sprinkle chicken with pepper.
Add chicken to nonstick skillet (sprayed with Lite cooking spray). Cook, turning until brown on all sides.
Sprinkle with garlic powder and cook one minute longer.
Add Italian dressing and soy sauce.
Sprinkle on brown sugar and curry.
Cover and cook over low heat for about 45 minutes or until chicken is done.

SERVES: 6

FAT GRAMS PER SERVING: 3

Nutritional Analysis Per Serving:

cal	*g. fat*	*(% of cal)*	*g.fib*	*mg. chol*	*mg. sod*
185	*3.08*	*15*	*0.63*	*67*	*4351*

SPAGHETTI MEATBALLS

1 1/2 cups fat free bread crumbs
1 cup skim milk
1 1/2 pounds ground turkey breast
8 ounces fat free egg substitute
1 medium onion, finely chopped
1/2 teaspoon allspice
1/4 teaspoon nutmeg
1 can fat free beef broth
3/4 teaspoon dill weed
1/4 teaspoon pepper

METHOD:

Soak bread crumbs in milk 5 minutes.
Combine crumb mixture with meat, egg and next four ingredients. Shape into balls about 2 inches in diameter. In Nonstick skillet, brown meatballs.
Place meatballs in slow cooker and add broth, dill weed and pepper. Cook on low 4 hours.

SERVES: 6

FAT GRAMS PER SERVING: FAT FREE

NOTE: N. analysis does NOT include apple syrup.

Nutritional Analysis Per Serving:

cal	g. fat	(%of cal)	g.fib	mg.chol	mg. sod
161	0.27	2	3.15	14	1187

SPAGHETTI, SOUTHERN STYLE

1 pound ground sirloin
4 ounces fat free egg substitute
1/2 onion, cut fine
1/4 cup fat free bread crumbs
1/4 teaspoon salt
2 tablespoons water
1/2 clove garlic, cut fine
1 teaspoon parsley, cut fine
Pinch of black pepper

METHOD:

Mix thoroughly and form into balls.
Brown in sprayed Nonstick skillet.
In sauce pan prepare the following:

SPAGHETTI SAUCE:

Pinch of black pepper
1/2 small onion, cut fine
Pinch of baking soda
1 tablespoon fat free margarine
1 6-ounce can tomato paste
1 1/2 cups water
1 teaspoon sugar

SERVES: 6

FAT GRAMS PER SERVING: 6

Nutritional Analysis Per Serving:

cal	*g. fat*	*(% of cal)*	*g.fib*	*mg. chol*	*mg. sod*
474	*5.51*	*10*	*6.72*	*52*	*371*

TURKEY-N-NOODLES

10 ounces medium noodles, flat eggless
16 ounces fat free sour cream
1 10 1/2-ounce can mushroom soup
1 can skim milk
1 medium onion
3 cloves garlic
Salt and pepper to taste
1 pound ground turkey breast
4 ounces fat free margarine

METHOD:

Cook noodles, drain.
Brown onions, garlic and meat.
Add water and cook until tender.
Stir together cream of mushroom soup and sour cream.
Mix noodles, meat and mixture together.
Use a sprayed glass oblong dish.
After putting mixture into dish, pat with fat free margarine then heat until bubbly hot.

SERVES: 6

FAT GRAMS PER SERVING: 4

Nutritional Analysis Per Serving:

cal	*g. fat*	*(%of cal)*	*g.fib*	*mg.chol*	*mg. sod*
324	*4.43*	*12*	*3.30*	*15*	*585*

Addiction

There are a lot of addicts in the world today. Habits that are so strong, that they have a control over some of us.

When we think of addicts, we generally think in terms of drugs, alcohol and smoking, but the list of addictions goes on:

coffee, soft drinks, chocolate, sweets, food, TV, sex, gambling, shopping, clothes, money, cars, horoscopes, sports, and the list doesn't end.

As you can see, they aren't all that evil, but they may still have a control over us.

Some may do more damage than others, but like sin, in The Good Book, liars are just as bad as murderers.If people will take the log out of their own eye, and then they will see clearly to take the speck out of their brother's eye.

Our problem is that some addictions are easier to see than others, which makes them easier to judge.

Maybe we need to walk in their shoes for awhile.

"COUNT YOUR BLESSINGS, NAME THEM ONE BY ONE."

HOT TAMALE PIE

3 cups boiling water
1 cup corn meal
1 pound ground turkey breast
1 onion, chopped
2 cups canned tomatoes
1 teaspoon salt
1/2 teaspoon pepper
1 tablespoon chili powder
1 teaspoon cumin seed

METHOD:

Sift corn meal slowly into boiling water, stirring constantly. Cook for 15 minutes.
Brown meat, onion and pepper in Nonstick skillet for 10 minutes.
Spray casserole dish, alternate layers of mush and meat. Bake in 400 degree oven for 20 minutes.

SERVES: 6

FAT GRAMS PER SERVING: 1

Nutritional Analysis Per Serving:

cal	*g. fat*	*(% of cal)*	*g.fib*	*mg. chol*	*mg. sod*
131	*0.71*	*5*	*1.59*	*9*	*272*

HONEY CHICKEN

4 boneless skinless chicken breasts
1/4 cup honey
3 tablespoons lemon juice
1 teaspoon Accent
4 ounces egg substitute
2 tablespoons soy sauce
1/4 teaspoon nutmeg

METHOD:

Line a baking pan with aluminum foil.
Arrange chicken in pan.
Stir together honey, egg, lemon juice, soy sauce, Accent and nutmeg.
Pour sauce over chicken, turning pieces to coat.
Bake, uncovered, in 350 degree oven for one hour or until done, turning and basting once.

SERVES: 4

FAT GRAMS PER SERVING: 3

Nutritional Analysis Per Serving:

cal	g. fat	(%of cal)	g.fib	mg.chol	mg. sod
261	3.07	11	0.27	67	1806

TOMATO DISH

1/2 cup skim milk
2 tablespoons fat free margarine
pepper
3/4 cup fat free salad dressing
1/2 cup onion, chopped
1 1/2 cup Lite Bisquick
3-4 fresh tomatoes
1 cup fat free sour cream
1 cup grated fat free cheese
1 pound ground turkey breast, cooked
1 teaspoon paprika

METHOD:

Combine milk and biscuit mix; stir to a soft dough.
Beat until stiff; knead 8 to 10 times on floured board.
Roll out to fit 9x9-inch pan.
Brush dough with melted margarine.
Cut tomatoes in wedges; arrange in rows over dough.
Sprinkle with pepper.
Combine sour cream, salad dressing, cheese, meat and onion; spoon over tomatoes.
Sprinkle with paprika.
Bake at 425 degrees for 10 minutes.
Reduce heat to 350 degrees and bake 15 to 20 minutes longer.

SERVES: 6

FAT GRAMS PER SERVING: 2

Nutritional Analysis Per Serving:

cal	*g. fat*	*(%of cal)*	*g.fib*	*mg.chol*	*mg. sod*
290	*2.29*	*7*	*0.25*	*17*	*1117*

TEXAS TURKEYBURGERS

3 pound ground turkey breast
3 cups tomato catsup
3 cups tomato puree
1 1/2 cups fresh tomatoes
2 1/2 tablespoons chili powder
1 teaspoon Tabasco sauce
1/2 teaspoon cayenne pepper
1 teaspoon black pepper
5 bay leaves
2 tablespoons thyme
3/4 cup brown sugar
1 clove garlic, chopped
2 large onions, chopped

METHOD:

Combine all ingredients (except ground turkey) and let simmer for 3 hours.
Form and cook turkeyburgers.
Place in sauce and let simmer until you are ready to serve.

SERVES: 12

FAT GRAMS PER SERVING: 1

Nutritional Analysis Per Serving:

cal	*g. fat*	*(% of cal)*	*g.fib*	*mg. chol*	*mg. sod*
294	*1.12*	*3*	*4.91*	*13*	*2219*

Good Books?

Have you read a "good book" lately?

A good book is generally one that agrees with you. Some people will read a good book several times. People will watch the same movies over and over. The same is true for plays, musicals and songs. TV holiday specials run year after year. According to sales figures, the Bible must be a good book. Most homes and motels have at least one. Some homes have several. If It is a good book, and It is, I wonder why people haven't read It all the way through at least once? The Bible is the Word of God. It is truth, life, light, love, exciting, alive and a whole lot more. You shouldn't judge a book if you haven't read it. You shouldn't judge the Bible by reading only a part of It. The Bible has sixty-six books within It. Don't base your opinion on what others say. Read it yourself.

TURKEY STROGANOFF

2 pounds ground turkey breast
2 medium onions, chopped
2 cloves garlic, minced
1/2 pound mushrooms, sliced
2 teaspoons salt
1/4 teaspoon pepper
1 tablespoon Worcestershire sauce
3 tablespoons tomato paste
1 cup fat free beef broth
1 cup fat free sour cream

METHOD:

In nonstick skillet cook turkey, discarding fat.
Combine all ingredients except sour cream in slow cooker.
Cook on low 3-4 hours.
Before serving, add sour cream to sauce and heat.

SERVES: 6

FAT GRAMS PER SERVING: 1

Nutritional Analysis Per Serving:

cal	*g. fat*	*(% of cal)*	*g.fib*	*mg. chol*	*mg. sod*
137	*0.52*	*3*	*2.08*	*23*	*803*

PASTAS/
GRAINS

INDEX TO PASTAS & GRAINS

AMISH CASSEROLE BREAD

1 package active dry yeast
1/4 cup lukewarm water
1 cup heated fat free cottage cheese (lukewarm)
2 tablespoons sugar
1 tablespoon fat free margarine
1 teaspoon salt
4 ounces fat free egg substitute
1 tablespoon minced onion
2 teaspoons dill seed
1/4 teaspoon soda
2 1/4 cups all-purpose flour

METHOD:

Soften yeast in lukewarm water.
Combine in a mixing bowl with the next 8 ingredients; mix well.
Gradually add flour until stiff dough is formed, beating well after each addition and increasing flour to 2 1/2 cups if necessary.
Cover; let rise in warm place until lite and doubled, 50-60 minutes.
Stir down; turn into well-greased 2-quart casserole dish.
Let rise again until lite, 30-40 minutes.
Bake at 350 degrees for 40-50 minutes, until golden brown.
Brush with soft margarine; sprinkle with salt.

NOTE: KNEADING IMPROVES LITENESS.

SERVES: 10

FAT GRAMS PER SERVING: FAT FREE

Nutritional Analysis Per Serving:

cal	*g. fat*	*(% of cal)*	*g.fib*	*mg. chol*	*mg. sod*
129	*0.31*	*2*	*0.80*	*1*	*210*

Receive

The Good Book says, "It is more blessed to give than to receive."

There sure isn't anything wrong with receiving. If you have ever had a need, it sure was a blessing when someone met the need.

We need to learn to receive and not feel like we can't take help. That is pride and we know God hates pride.

It is not as easy for some people to receive as it is for some to give. God wants us to learn to receive so that we can receive all that He has for us.

He wants us to see Him as our source and learn to realize that He gives out of His love for us. Stop and think how important receivers are the next time someone wants to help and you feel like you can't receive.

Number one, God may be using them to answer your prayers so don't shut it off.

Number two, how could it ever be possible for anyone to be more blessed, if there were no receivers in this world.

BANANA BREAD

1 8-ounce tub fat free margarine
1/2 cup Lite brown sugar
1/2 cup white sugar
4 ounces fat free egg substitute
1 teaspoon vanilla
2 1/2 very ripe bananas, mashed
1 1/2 cups presifted flour
1 teaspoon baking powder
1/3 cup low fat buttermilk, mixed with
1/2 teaspoon baking soda
1/2 cup Grape Nuts Cereal

METHOD:

Beat margarine and sugar together until fluffy; add fat free egg substitute and vanilla.
Beat well.
Add mashed bananas; beat again.
Alternately add flour, , baking powder and buttermilk mixture.
Add 1/2 cup Grape Nuts cereal.
Pour into sprayed and floured loaf pan; bake at 325 degrees until golden brown and soft to touch.

SERVES: 8

FAT GRAMS PER SERVING: 1

Nutritional Analysis Per Serving:

cal	*g. fat*	*(% of cal)*	*g.fib*	*mg. chol*	*mg. sod*
248	*0.63*	*2*	*2.86*	*1*	*376*

BROCCOLI CORN BREAD

1 10 1/2-ounce package frozen chopped broccoli
8 ounces fat free egg substitute
1 8-ounce cup fat free cottage cheese
1 onion, chopped
1 8 1/2-ounce box Jiffy corn bread mix
4 ounces fat free margarine

METHOD:

Melt margarine in 9x12-inch pan.
Mix ingredients together.
Cook at 350 degrees for 30 minutes.

SERVES: 8

FAT GRAMS PER SERVING: 3

Nutritional Analysis Per Serving:

cal	*g. fat*	*(%of cal)*	*g.fib*	*mg.chol*	*mg. sod*
209	*3.29*	*14*	*1.94*	*3*	*631*

BUTTERMILK CORN BREAD

2 cups corn meal
1 teaspoon salt
1 teaspoon soda
2 cups low fat buttermilk
4 ounces fat free egg substitute
1/4 cup applesauce

METHOD:

Combine corn meal, salt and soda.
Combine buttermilk, fat free egg substitute and applesauce.
Add to dry ingredients.
Pour into hot well-sprayed muffin pans, corn stick pans or 10-inch sprayed iron skillet.
Bake in hot oven (450 degrees) for 20 minutes for muffins or corn sticks and 25 to 30 minutes in iron skillet.

SERVES: 12

FAT GRAMS PER SERVING: 1

Nutritional Analysis Per Serving:

cal	*g. fat*	*(% of cal)*	*g.fib*	*mg. chol*	*mg. sod*
110	*0.79*	*6*	*0.07*	*2*	*163*

CHARLESTON RICE

1 teaspoon fat free margarine
1/2 cup chopped celery
1 2 1/2-ounce can mushrooms
1/2 teaspoon poultry seasoning
1/2 teaspoon celery seed
4 ounces fat free egg substitute
1/2 cup chopped onions
1/2 cup chopped green pepper
3 cups cooked rice
1/2 teaspoon salt
1/4 teaspoon pepper

METHOD:

In Nonstick skillet melt margarine, add onions, green pepper and celery.
Cook until tender.
Add drained and chopped mushrooms, cooked rice, poultry seasoning, salt, celery seed, pepper and then stir in beaten fat free egg substitute.
Turn out into a sprayed dish or casserole dish and cover.
Bake in 350 degree oven for 15 minutes.

SERVES: 4

FAT GRAMS PER SERVING: FAT FREE

Nutritional Analysis Per Serving:

cal	*g. fat*	*(%of cal)*	*g.fib*	*mg.chol*	*mg. sod*
229	*0.46*	*2*	*1.21*	*0*	*201*

CHEESE GRITS

1 1/2 cups grits
7 cups water
1 pound fat free sharp cheese, grated
8 ounces fat free fat free egg substitute
1 tablespoon Worcestershire sauce
1 garlic bud, pressed
4 ounces fat free margarine
1 dash of Tabasco sauce

METHOD:

Cook grits in water until thick.
Add remainder of ingredients and bake in casserole for 45 minutes (about 350 degrees).

SERVES: 8

FAT GRAMS PER SERVING: FAT FREE

Nutritional Analysis Per Serving:

cal	g. fat	(% of cal)	g.fib	mg. chol	mg. sod
481	0.35	1	0.47	32	1887

CORN SPOON BREAD

8 ounces fat free egg substitute
1 8 1/2-ounce package corn muffin mix
1 8-ounce can cream style corn
1 8-ounce package frozen whole kernel corn
1 cup fat free sour cream
1/2 cup fat free margarine, melted
1 4-ounce cup shredded fat free process Swiss cheese

METHOD:

Combine fat free egg substitute, muffin mix, cream-style corn, whole kernel corn, sour cream and margarine.
Spread in 11x7x1 3/4-inch baking dish.
Bake in 350 degree oven for 35 minutes.
Sprinkle cheese on top; bake 10 or 15 minutes more, until knife comes out clean.

SERVES: 8

FAT GRAMS PER SERVING: 3

Nutritional Analysis Per Serving:

cal	*g. fat*	*(%of cal)*	*g.fib*	*mg.chol*	*mg. sod*
276	*3.44*	*11*	*1.56*	*4*	*682*

Mail?

Did you read your mail today? It is always exciting to get mail, especially when it is from a loved one.

Well, God has sent us mail. With His mail, we can have mail to read everyday.

No days off for delivery. It never gets delayed by bad weather. Never lost. Never sent back for postage due. You can even pick out what kind of letter you want.

Looking for peace, encouragement, love, direction, help, counsel, wisdom, hope, or whatever else you desire?

Whatever the subject, God has the answer in His letters to us (you and me). I think that on some of God's mail, He has put a P.S., "Haven't heard from you lately."

God wants to hear from us too. Why don't you write a love letter to God. How do you write to God? His address is on the house of those whom He dwells in.

Pass His love on. Everyone likes to get mail. Jesus said, "When we did it to others, we did it to Him."

FRUIT BREAD

2 cups all-purpose flour
1 cup sugar
1 1/2 teaspoons baking powder
1 teaspoon salt
1/2 teaspoon baking soda
2 tablespoons applesauce
1 tablespoon grated orange peel
3/4 cup orange juice
4 ounces fat free egg substitute
1 cup fresh cranberries, coarsely chopped
1/2 cup Grape Nuts cereal

METHOD:

Preheat oven to 350 degrees.
Mix together flour, sugar, baking powder, salt and baking soda.
Stir in orange juice, orange peel, applesauce and fat free egg substitute. Mix until well blended.
Stir in cranberries and nuts.
Turn into a 9x5-inch loaf pan, sprayed on bottom only.
Bake 55 minutes, or until toothpick inserted in center comes out clean.
Cool thoroughly before serving.

SERVES: 8

FAT GRAMS PER SERVING: FAT FREE

Nutritional Analysis Per Serving:

cal	*g. fat*	*(%of cal)*	*g.fib*	*mg.chol*	*mg. sod*
218	*0.45*	*2*	*2.53*	*0.00*	*300*

HOT MEXICAN CORNBREAD

1 cup yellow corn meal
1 cup skim milk with 1/2 teaspoon soda
1 teaspoon salt
2 jalapeno peppers, chopped fine
1 15 1/4-ounce can cream style corn
4 ounces fat free egg substitute
1 cup green onions, minced (scallions)
1/2 pound grated fat free Cheddar cheese
1/4 cup applesauce

METHOD:

Mix together all ingredients, reserve half the cheese for topping.
Spray nonstick skillet and heat until hot.
Pour mixture into sprayed hot iron skillet and top with remaining cheese.
Bake at 350 degrees for 40 minutes.

SERVES: 8

FAT GRAMS PER SERVING: 1

Nutritional Analysis Per Serving:

cal	*g. fat*	*(% of cal)*	*g.fib*	*mg. chol*	*mg. sod*
373	*1.13*	*3*	*1.24*	*16*	*990*

INDIANA RICE

2 1/2 cups cooked rice
1 1/2 cups evaporated skim milk
2/3 cup Lite brown sugar
3 tablespoons fat free margarine
8 ounces fat free egg substitute, beaten
1 teaspoon vanilla
1/2 teaspoon nutmeg
1/2 teaspoon cinnamon
1/2 cup raisins

METHOD:

Spray (Lite cooking spray) cooker well.
Combine all ingredients in cooker and mix thoroughly.
Cook on low 4-6 hours, or on automatic 3 hours.

SERVES: 6

FAT GRAMS PER SERVING: FAT FREE

Nutritional Analysis Per Serving:

cal	*g. fat*	*(%of cal)*	*g.fib*	*mg.chol*	*mg. sod*
277	*0.40*	*1*	*0.88*	*2*	*181*

MACARONI & CHEESE SOUFFLE

2 cups macaroni, cooked
1 1/2 cup scalded skim milk
1 1/2 cup soft fat free bread crumbs
1/2 pound grated fat free American cheese
6 ounces fat free egg substitute
1/4 cup chopped pimento
3 tablespoons melted fat free margarine
1 tablespoon chopped parsley
1 tablespoon grated onion
3 egg whites
1/4 teaspoon cream of tartar

METHOD:

Pour hot milk over bread crumbs.
Add 1 1/2 cups cheese, cover and let stand until cheese melts. Add macaroni, fat free egg substitute, pimento, margarine, parsley, and onion.
Beat egg whites with cream of tartar until stiff but not dry and fold into macaroni mixture.
Pour into a baking dish and set in a shallow pan and fill to 1 inch with hot water. Bake at 350 degrees for 45 to 60 minutes.
Cover with the remaining cheese and melt.

SERVES: 6

FAT GRAMS PER SERVING: FAT FREE

Nutritional Analysis Per Serving:

cal	*g. fat*	*(% of cal)*	*g.fib*	*mg. chol*	*mg. sod*
204	*0.42*	*2*	*1.07*	*6*	*704*

MACARONI SUPREME

1 pound lean ground sirloin
1/2 cup fat free salad dressing
30 ounce jar fat free spaghetti sauce
1 7-ounce package macaroni (cooked)
3/4 cup shredded, cheddar fat free cheese

METHOD:

Brown meat and drain.
Combine all ingredients in sprayed nonstick skillet.
Heat on medium stirring occasionally.
Top with fat free cheese.

SERVES: 6

FAT GRAMS PER SERVING:3

Nutritional Analysis Per Serving:

cal	*g. fat*	*(%of cal)*	*g.fib*	*mg.chol*	*mg. sod*
354	*3.04*	*7*	*5.33*	*37*	*1170*

NUT BREAD

2 cups sifted all-purpose flour
3/4 cup granulated sugar
3 teaspoons baking powder
1/2 teaspoon baking soda
1 teaspoon cinnamon
1 cup Grape Nuts cereal
4 ounces fat free egg substitute
1 cup Whole Cranberry Sauce, drained
2 tablespoons applesauce

METHOD:

Heat oven to 350 degrees.
Sift together the flour, sugar, baking powder, soda and cinnamon.
Add Grape Nuts cereal.
In mixing bowl, beat egg; add cranberry sauce and applesauce.
Add dry ingredients; stir until just blended.
Pour into greased 9x5x3-inch loaf pan.
Bake in 350 degree oven 45 minutes.
Cool on rack.

SERVES: 8

FAT GRAMS PER SERVING: FAT FREE

Nutritional Analysis Per Serving:

cal	*g. fat*	*(% of cal)*	*g.fib*	*mg. chol*	*mg. sod*
295	*0.47*	*1*	*3.87*	*0.00*	*370*

OLD-FASHIONED CORN BREAD

2 cups yellow corn meal
1 cup all-purpose flour
1 cup fat free sour cream
3 tablespoons baking powder
4 ounces fat free egg substitute
1 cup cream style corn
1 1/2 teaspoon salt
1/2 cup applesauce
Skim milk

METHOD:

Mix all ingredients together until well blended.
Add enough milk to make the mixture pour easily.
Fill muffin tins 1/2 full.
Place in preheated 400 degree oven until golden brown, about 20 to 30 minutes.

SERVES: 24

FAT GRAMS PER SERVING: FAT FREE

Nutritional Analysis Per Serving:

cal	*g. fat*	*(%of cal)*	*g.fib*	*mg.chol*	*mg. sod*
87	*0.21*	*2*	*0.30*	*1.38*	*250*

Mothers

Many look at a woman in a business suit, carrying a briefcase and think, there goes a successful business woman.

They may be right and she may be, but why can't we say the same thing about a mother carrying a child or with a car full of children.

She has the responsibility of raising our future generation of leaders, doctors, teachers, mothers, worker and so on.

We tend to think of being a mother as someone who could not find a good job. In a sense, they may be right. Her job is seven days a week.

On call for twenty-four hours a day. No holidays off. No great appreciation for what she does. Then after twenty or so years, who needs her unless it may be to baby-sit the grandchildren. Being a full-time mother is not an easy job.

We need to spend more time looking up to mothers instead of in the other direction. You wouldn't be here without her.

POTATOES AU GRATIN (MICROWAVE)

4 medium potatoes
1/4 cup fat free margarine
1/4 cup all-purpose flour
2 teaspoons snipped chives
1 teaspoon salt
1/2 teaspoon dry mustard
1/8 teaspoon pepper
1 3/4 cups skim milk
1 cup shredded fat free Cheddar cheese

METHOD:

Pierce potatoes and arrange on microwave-safe paper towel in oven. Cook on full power for 10 to 14 minutes, or until done.
Turn potatoes over halfway through cooking time.
Set aside to cool.
Place butter in 2-quart casserole dish. Heat on full power for 45 seconds to 1 minute 15 seconds, or until melted.
Stir in flour, chives, salt, dry mustard and pepper.
Gradually stir in milk.
Cook, covered, on full power for 5 to 8 minutes, or until thickened.
Stir occasionally during cooking time.
Stir in cheese.
Slice potatoes and add to sauce.
Heat, covered, on full power for 3 1/2 to 5 1/2 minutes, or until cheese is melted and potatoes are heated through.

SERVES: 4-6

FAT GRAMS PER SERVING: FAT FREE

Nutritional Analysis Per Serving:

cal	*g. fat*	*(%of cal)*	*g.fib*	*mg.chol*	*mg. sod*
162	*0.33*	*2*	*1.86*	*4*	*379*

GROUND BEEF STROGANOFF FOR TWO

1/2 pound lean ground beef
1/4 cup chopped onion
4 1/2 teaspoons all-purpose flour
1/2 teaspoon salt
1/8 teaspoon garlic powder
1/2 teaspoon instant beef flavored bouillon
1/2 cup hot tap water
2 tablespoons catsup
1/4 cup fat free dairy sour cream
2 cups cooked egg noodles

METHOD:

Combine beef and onion in 1-quart casserole dish.
Cook, covered, on full power for 2 1/2 to 3 1/2 minutes, or until beef is no longer pink and onion is tender.
Stir halfway through cooking time. Drain.
Add flour, salt and garlic powder.
Dissolve bouillon in hot water and add to beef. Add catsup.
Cook, covered on full power for 2 1/2 to 4 minutes, or until simmering.
Stir halfway through cooking time.
Stir in sour cream.
Serve over warm, cooked noodles.

SERVES: 4

FAT GRAMS PER SERVING: 2

Nutritional Analysis Per Serving:

cal	*g. fat*	*(% of cal)*	*g.fib*	*mg. chol*	*mg. sod*
207	*2.32*	*10*	*1.87*	*28*	*488*

PUMPKIN BREAD

3 cups sugar
1 cup applesauce
8 ounces fat free egg substitute
1 16-ounce can pumpkin
1 1/2 cups flour
2 teaspoons baking soda
1 teaspoon baking powder
1 teaspoon nutmeg
1 teaspoon Allspice
1 teaspoon cloves
2/3 cup water

METHOD:

Cream sugar and applesauce.
Add eggs and pumpkin; mix well.
Add dry ingredients alternately with water.
Pour into 2 well sprayed and floured 9x5 loaf pans.
Bake at 350 degrees for 1 1/2 hours or until done.
Let stand 10 minutes until cool.
Makes two loaves.

SERVES: 12

FAT GRAMS PER SERVING: FAT FREE

Nutritional Analysis Per Serving:

cal	*g. fat*	*(%of cal)*	*g.fib*	*mg.chol*	*mg. sod*
171	*0.48*	*3*	*2.92*	*0.19*	*135*

SHRIMP EGGPLANT DRESSING

1 eggplant
1/2 cup celery, chopped
1 bell pepper, chopped
1 cup rice
1 pound raw shrimp

METHOD:

Cook rice as directed.
Boil eggplant until tender.
Add onions, celery and raw shrimp.
Salt and pepper.
Let simmer on low heat until cooked (approximately) 20 to 30 minutes.
Add more salt and pepper if needed.
Now add cooked rice and cover and let simmer 10 to 15 minutes.

SERVES: 6

FAT GRAMS PER SERVING: 2

Nutritional Analysis Per Serving:

cal	*g. fat*	*(% of cal)*	*g.fib*	*mg. chol*	*mg. sod*
245	*1.83*	*7*	*4.91*	*115*	*133*

SPAGHETTI BAKE (MICROWAVE)

1/3 cup sliced green onion
1/4 cup chopped green pepper
1 4-ounce can sliced mushrooms, drained
2 tablespoons fat free margarine
1 1/2 cups (12 ounce) fat free cottage cheese
1/2 cup fat free sour cream
1/4 cup grated fat free Parmesan cheese
1/4 teaspoon pepper
8 ounces spaghetti, cooked and drained
1 cup shredded fat free Cheddar cheese

METHOD:

Combine green onion, green pepper, mushrooms and margarine in 3-quart casserole dish.
Cook, covered, on full power for 2 1/2 to 4 1/2 minutes, or until green onion and green pepper are tender.
Stir halfway through cooking time.
Stir in cottage cheese, sour cream, Parmesan cheese, pepper, cooked spaghetti, and cheddar cheese.
Mix well.
Heat, covered, on full power for 5 1/2 minutes, or until cheese is melted.

SERVES: 6

FAT GRAMS PER SERVING: 1

Nutritional Analysis Per Serving:

cal	*g. fat*	*(%of cal)*	*g.fib*	*mg.chol*	*mg. sod*
257	*0.64*	*2*	*0.42*	*8*	*535*

SOUPS AND SALADS

SOUPS & SALADS INDEX

Liked?

We all like to be liked. But it is more important to be liked by those that are important to us.
The peer-pressure group that comes from our age group, or those that we want to be like . We will sometimes do almost anything to be accepted by them.
It may hurt others, but it is O.K. if it pleases the right people. God isn't that way.
He takes us just as we are. All that He wants us to do is to believe in Him.
God loved us while we were still doing lots of dumb things. He was just waiting around for us to say that we loved Him too.
The people that we try to please will change. Their likes and dislikes will change. God won't change.
What God likes and hates won't change. His love won't change.
Over the years, your best friends may change, or move, or die.
Your likes will change and not even be as important as before. God won't change, move, or No big survey taken, but the other day I had the opportunity to hold the door open several times for different people.
I wasn't totally amazed, but some what, by the number of people who walk through the door without a smile or thank you.
Such a simple thing but many have forgotten the word, thank you. I guess now I understand why many have forgotten the word, thank you.
I guess now I understand why many people don't hold the door for other people. After awhile, you develop the attitude of why bother, no one cares anymore.
I wonder if God sometimes feel that way?
The Good Books says, "In everything gives thanks: for this is God's will for you in Christ."

BEAN SOUP

1 pound Mr. Turkey polish sausage
2 cups dried beans
2 tablespoons rice
2 stalks celery, sliced
2 medium potatoes, cubed
2 cups undrained tomatoes
1/4 teaspoon pepper
1/2 cup dried split peas
2 tablespoons barley
2 onions, sliced
1 cup diced turnip
1 teaspoon salt

METHOD:

Wash beans, drain, add fresh water.
In large kettle soak beans, peas, rice and barley overnight in water to cover.
Bring to boil in same water.
Add remaining ingredients and simmer for one hour.
Add one pound Mr. Turkey polish sausage.
Simmer for 2 hours or until done.

SERVES: 12

FAT GRAMS PER SERVING: 1

Nutritional Analysis Per Serving:

cal	*g. fat*	*(%of cal)*	*g.fib*	*mg.chol*	*mg. sod*
194	*1.49*	*7*	*6.01*	*16.67*	*568*

BLUEBERRY SALAD

2 0.6-ounce packages sugar free blackberry Jell-O
1 21-ounce can Lite blueberries, drained
1 20-ounce can crushed pineapple
1 cup Grape Nuts cereal
2 cups boiling water
2 cups lite cool whip

METHOD:

Dissolve Jell-O in water; cool.
Add pineapple and juice of berries; chill and allow partially to set.
Add Grape Nuts cereal and berries.
Fold in cool whip.
Chill until set.

SERVES: 12

FAT GRAMS PER SERVING: 2

Nutritional Analysis Per Serving:

cal	*g. fat*	*(% of cal)*	*g.fib*	*mg. chol*	*mg. sod*
207	*1.57*	*7*	*2.62*	*0.00*	*213*

CABBAGE SALAD

1 0.3-ounce package unflavored gelatin
1/4 cup sugar
3 tablespoons white vinegar
1 cup cold water
1 cup celery
1 tablespoon pimento
1/2 cup cold water
1/2 teaspoon salt
1 tablespoon lemon juice
1/2 cup cabbage
1 tablespoon green pepper

METHOD:

In small pan combine gelatin and 1 cup cold water.
Place over low heat and stir constantly until gelatin dissolves, about 3 minutes. Remove from heat.
Add sugar, salt, vinegar, lemon juice and 1/2 cup cold water.
Stir until sugar is dissolved.
Cool in refrigerator until the consistency of uncooked egg whites.
Finely chop cabbage, celery, pepper and pimento.
Fold vegetables into gelatin mixture.
Litely spray a 3-cup mold and spoon salad into mold.
Chill until firm.

SERVES: 4

FAT GRAMS PER SERVING: FAT FREE

Nutritional Analysis Per Serving:

cal	*g. fat*	*(%of cal)*	*g.fib*	*mg.chol*	*mg. sod*
29	*0.08*	*2*	*0.65*	*0.00*	*127*

CABBAGE SOUP

1 46-ounce can tomato juice
2 tablespoons instant minced onion
2 10 1/2-ounce cans fat free instant beef broth
2 cups shredded cabbage
7 tablespoons lemon juice
1/2 cup water
1/2 teaspoon oregano
1 tablespoon sugar

METHOD:

Combine juices, water, onion, broth and herbs.
Bring to a boil.
Add cabbage and cover.
Simmer 20 minutes.
Stir in sugar.

SERVES: 6

FAT GRAMS PER SERVING: FAT FREE

Nutritional Analysis Per Serving:

cal	*g. fat*	*(% of cal)*	*g.fib*	*mg. chol*	*mg. sod*
83	*0.23*	*2*	*0.67*	*7*	*2410*

CHAMPAGNE SALAD

1 8-ounce package fat free cream cheese
1 8-ounce package frozen strawberries, thawed
2 bananas, sliced
2 cups of lite cool whip
1 cup sugar
1 cup crushed pineapple, drained
1/2 cup Grape Nuts cereal

METHOD:

Mix cream cheese and sugar in mixer; add juice from strawberries.
Slowly Add all other ingredients.
Fold in whipped topping.
Turn into a 13x9-inch pan and freeze.
This can be refrozen.

SERVES: 9

FAT GRAMS PER SERVING: 2

Nutritional Analysis Per Serving:

cal	*g. fat*	*(%of cal)*	*g.fib*	*mg.chol*	*mg. sod*
189	*2.04*	*10*	*2.46*	*4*	*190*

CHERRY WALDORF SALAD

1 0.6-ounce package sugar free cherry Jello
1 cup cold water
1 1/2 cups chopped apples
1/2 cup Grape Nuts cereal
2 cups boiling water
1/3 cup lemon juice
1 cup chopped celery

METHOD:

Dissolve Jello in boiling water.
Add cold water and lemon juice.
Chill until slighty thickened.
Fold in apples, celery and Grape Nuts cereal.
Pour into 9-inch square baking dish and chill about 3 hours.

SERVES: 6

FAT GRAMS PER SERVING: FAT FREE

Nutritional Analysis Per Serving:

cal	*g. fat*	*(% of cal)*	*g.fib*	*mg. chol*	*mg. sod*
107	*0.28*	*2*	*3.03*	*0.00*	*234*

The Joy of a Child

The joy of a child at Christmas. The love of a family around a table overflowing with the tastiest of foods.

The lights and sounds of the holidays. Share your joy, or love, or time, or food, or clothing, or shelter with someone this holiday season.

Let God's love flow through you to someone in need. Ask God to show you what to do or who to help.

Jesus said, "Greater love has no one than this, that one would lay down his life for his friend." The laying down of your life is really the giving of yourself.

Maybe someone only needs someone to talk to - your time, or maybe it is something to eat - your food.

Don't get too busy this holiday season and miss out on the true meaning of Christmas. God gave us His Son, hopefully, we can give something of ourselves.

CHOWDER

1 cup chopped onion
1 clove crushed garlic
3 8-ounce cans tomato sauce
1/4 teaspoon thyme
Dash cayenne
1 1/2 chopped green pepper
1/4 cup raw rice
3 4-ounce cans shrimp
1 bay leaf
1 quart hot water
4 ounce fat free margarine

METHOD:

Saute onion, pepper and garlic in fat free margarine in a non-stick skillet.
In kettle combine onion mixture, tomato sauce rice, drained shrimp, bay leaf, thyme, water and cayenne.
Bring to a boil and simmer for one hour.

SERVES: 6

FAT GRAMS PER SERVING: 2

Nutritional Analysis Per Serving:

cal	*g. fat*	*(% of cal)*	*g.fib*	*mg. chol*	*mg. sod*
189	*1.60*	*8*	*4.18*	*98*	*1602*

COCA-COLA SALAD

1 16-ounce can dark sweet cherries
1 0.3-ounce package sugar free cherry Jello
2 tablespoons lemon juice
1 cup Diet Coca-Cola
1/2 cup Grape Nuts cereal
1 3-ounce package fat free cream cheese

METHOD:

Drain cherries and reserve juice.
Heat juice to boiling and remove from heat.
Add Jello and stir until dissolved.
Add Coca-Cola and lemon juice.
Chill until it mounds slightly.
Cut cheese into small pieces and fold into gelatin along with Grape Nuts cereal and drained cherries.
Spoon into mold and chill until set.

SERVES: 4

FAT GRAMS PER SERVING: FAT FREE

Nutritional Analysis Per Serving:

cal	*g. fat*	*(%of cal)*	*g.fib*	*mg.chol*	*mg. sod*
250	*0.17*	*1*	*3.80*	*3*	*341*

CORN SALAD

1 0.3-ounce package sugar free lemon Jello
1/2 teaspoon salt
3/4 cup cold water
1/3 cup diced celery
1 cup boiling water
2 teaspoons vinegar
1 cup frozen whole kernel corn
2 tablespoons diced green pepper

METHOD:

Cook frozen corn in water and cool
Dissolve Jello in boiling water.
Add salt, vinegar and cold water.
Chill until slitely thickened.
Fold in corn, celery and pepper.
Pour into 3-cup mold and chill.
Unmold and garnish with greens.

SERVES: 4

FAT GRAMS PER SERVING: FAT FREE

Nutritional Analysis Per Serving:

cal	*g. fat*	*(% of cal)*	*g.fib*	*mg. chol*	*mg. sod*
57	*0.37*	*6*	*0.52*	*0.00*	*167*

Empty Feelings?

Holidays are over.

The gifts have been opened. Most family and friends have gone to their homes. The biggest holidays of the year are over and then comes the big let-down feeling.

You aren't sure why, but for some reason, you feel a little sad...

You may have a kind of an empty feeling inside. That is what happens a lot of the time when we set goals, and after they are achieved, there comes an emptiness.

We thought "it" (the goal) would bring everlasting happiness or joy. But the happiness never last to long before we seem to have the need to set new goals so we can be happy again. Always chasing that pot of gold at the end of the rainbow.

The Good Book says that we are to seek Him, make Him our goal and He will give us eternal life. Life abundantly - love, joy, peace and rest. Are you setting lasting goals?

COUNTRY CHICKEN CHOWDER

6 boneless skinless cooked chicken breasts
1/2 cup chopped onion
2 tablespoons fat free margarine
1 10 1/2-ounce can condensed cream of chicken soup
1/2 soup can water
1 15-1/4 ounce frozen package cream style yellow corn
1 12-ounce can evaporated skim milk
1/4 teaspoon pepper
2 tablespoons chopped parsley
1 cup shredded fat free cheese

METHOD:

Boil chicken until done.
Break into small pieces.
Saute onions in margarine until limp.
Do not brown.
Combine all ingredients, except parsley.
Simmer 15 to 20 minutes or until real bubbly.
Sprinkle with cheese and garnish with parsley.

SERVES: 6

FAT GRAMS PER SERVING: 7

Nutritional Analysis Per Serving:

cal	*g. fat*	*(% of cal)*	*g.fib*	*mg. chol*	*mg. sod*
388	*7.09*	*16*	*1.24*	*76*	*785*

CRANBERRY SALAD

3 ounce package sugar free orange Jello
3 ounce package sugar free cherry Jello
1 cup hot water
1 pound can whole berry cranberry sauce
15 ounce can crushed pineapple, undrained
6 ounce can orange juice, concentrate
8 ounces Grape Nuts cereal

METHOD:

Dissolve orange and cherry Jello in hot water, add remaining ingredients and mix well.
Prepare 6 cup ring mold with Lite spray.
Pour in mold and chill until firm.
You can just pour in bowl.
For mold add 1 envelope Knox gelatin.

SERVES: 12

FAT GRAMS PER SERVING: FAT FREE

Nutritional Analysis Per Serving:

cal	*g. fat*	*(%of cal)*	*g.fib*	*mg.chol*	*mg. sod*
391	*0.36*	*1*	*6.77*	*0.00*	*479*

CREAM CHEESE SALAD

1 0.3-ounce sugar free package cherry Jell-O
1 21-ounce can Lite cherry pie filling
1/2 cup diced celery
1 0.3-ounce sugar free package lemon Jell-O
1 8-ounce package fat free cream cheese
1 20-ounce can crushed pineapple, undrained

METHOD:

Dissolve 1 package cherry Jell-O and 1 cup boiling water; stir in cherry pie filling.
When cool, add 1/2 cup diced celery.
Place in mold or glass baking dish.
When set, add dry lemon Jello, cream cheese, and pineapple.
Mix well.
Layer on top.
Chill 2 or 3 hours.

SERVES: 6

FAT GRAMS PER SERVING: FAT FREE

Nutritional Analysis Per Serving:

cal	*g. fat*	*(% of cal)*	*g.fib*	*mg. chol*	*mg. sod*
414	*0.01*	*<1*	*3.70*	*5*	*348*

CREAM SALAD

1 0.3-ounce box lime Jell-O, mixed according to package directions
1 cup marshmallows
1 20-ounce can crushed pineapple, drained
8 ounces fat free cream cheese

METHOD:

Melt marshmallows and cream cheese; add to Jell-O.
Stir in pineapple; refrigerate.

SERVES: 6

FAT GRAMS PER SERVING: FAT FREE

Nutritional Analysis Per Serving:

cal	*g. fat*	*(%of cal)*	*g.fib*	*mg.chol*	*mg. sod*
383	*0.47*	*1*	*4.01*	*5*	*232*

Fantasy

Today, many people are living in a fantasy world. We had a TV series for awhile called Fantasy Island, where people went to live out their fantasy.

Many amusement parks have a fantasy land. Many women get caught up in the soap operas and men with their Playboy or other things to excite them.

When problems come, many people go off into a fantasy world rather than face them. It becomes an escape.

A place where everything works out the way that they want it. Some people do it so much that they can't separate the real from the fantasy.

Jesus says that He is the truth. There is a heaven and hell. The Good Books says, "I call heaven and earth to witness against you today, that I have set before you life and death, the blessing and the curse.

So choose life in order that you may live, you and your descendants." God is saying, "Wake up and learn what is really important in life." Then choose life in Him.

CROCKPOT CHILI

2 15-ounce cans chili beans
2 15-ounce cans tomato sauce
1 pound lean ground sirloin
4 tablespoons powdered cumin
1 tablespoon cayenne pepper
1/2 onion

METHOD:

Brown meat, drain well, and all other ingredients.
Simmer on low for 2-4 hours.
Remember to use fat free crackers.

SERVES: 9

FAT GRAMS PER SERVING: 4

Nutritional Analysis Per Serving:

cal	*g. fat*	*(%of cal)*	*g.fib*	*mg.chol*	*mg. sod*
291	*3.72*	*11*	*11.81*	*23*	*1180*

CUCUMBER SALAD

4 cucumbers, unpared
1 tablespoon salt
1/2 cup white vinegar
1/2 cup sugar
1/2 teaspoon pepper
2 tablespoons dried dill weed

METHOD:

Cut cucumber into thin slices and place in bowl with tight fitting lid.
Combine sugar, salt and pepper.
Sprinkle over cucumbers and cover.
Shake to coat cucumbers.
Add vinegar and cover.
Refrigerate at least 24 hours.
Sprinkle with dill at serving time.

SERVES: 4

FAT GRAMS PER SERVING: FAT FREE

Nutritional Analysis Per Serving:

cal	*g. fat*	*(% of cal)*	*g.fib*	*mg. chol*	*mg. sod*
41	*0.09*	*2*	*0.34*	*0.00*	*585*

CUCUMBERS DELITE

2 tablespoons sugar
Dash pepper
1/4 cup vinegar
1 cucumber, unpared
2 tablespoons chopped parsley
1 teaspoon salt
1 teaspoon celery seed
1 tablespoon lemon juice
1/4 cup onion

METHOD:

Combine sugar, salt, pepper, celery seed, vinegar, lemon juice in bowl.
Slice cucumber and add to vinegar mixture.
Add onion and parsley.
Chill.

SERVES: 2

FAT GRAMS PER SERVING: FAT FREE

Nutritional Analysis Per Serving:

cal	*g. fat*	*(%of cal)*	*g.fib*	*mg.chol*	*mg. sod*
35	*0.19*	*5*	*0.78*	*0.06*	*392*

EVANSVILLE'S CHILI

1 tablespoon fat free margarine
2 15-ounce cans kidney beans
1 1/2 teaspoon chili powder
1 1/2 teaspoon pepper
2 finely chopped onions
2 finely chopped green peppers
1 1/2 teaspoon flour
2 pounds ground turkey breast
1 3/4 pounds fresh tomatoes (cut up)
1 tablespoon fat free margarine
1 large clove garlic, crushed
1 1/2 teaspoons caraway seed spice

METHOD:

Brown turkey in margarine in nonstick skillet.
Put browned turkey in large pot.
Add beans, chili powder, salt, pepper.
Saute onions in 1 tablespoon margarine in nonstick skillet, then add garlic clove.
Add onion mixture to meat mixture in kettle.
Add green pepper.
Cook chili mixture for 45 minutes.
Just before cooking time is up add caraway spice mixture and stir well. Cook about 3 to 4 minutes longer.

SERVES: 12

FAT GRAMS PER SERVING: 1

Nutritional Analysis Per Serving:

cal	*g. fat*	*(% of cal)*	*g.fib*	*mg. chol*	*mg. sod*
180	*0.99*	*5*	*1.96*	*9*	*737*

FELLOWSHIP SALAD

1 cup diced onions
1 cup diced celery
1 10-ounce package frozen mixed vegetables
1 cup sugar
2 tablespoons flour or cooking starch
2 teaspoons salt
2 teaspoons prepared mustard
1/2 cup vinegar
1 cup water 1/2 teaspoon pepper

METHOD:

Cook frozen vegetables by package directions or until tender.
Mix sugar, flour, starch, vinegar and water.
Cook until thickened and clear.
Pour over vegetables.
Refrigerate overnight to marinate.
May add red mangos for color as well as taste.

SERVES: 4

FAT GRAMS PER SERVING: FAT FREE

Nutritional Analysis Per Serving:

cal	*g. fat*	*(%of cal)*	*g.fib*	*mg.chol*	*mg. sod*
99	***0.43***	***4***	***3.41***	***0.00***	***321***

FIVE-CUP SALAD

1 cup miniature marshmallows
1 cup mandarin oranges
1 cup pineapple tidbits
$^{1}/_{3}$ cup Angel Flake coconut
1 cup fat free sour cream

METHOD:

Mix all ingredients, refrigerate.
Let stand overnight.

SERVES: 6

FAT GRAMS PER SERVING: 2

Nutritional Analysis Per Serving:

cal	*g. fat*	*(% of cal)*	*g.fib*	*mg. chol*	*mg. sod*
162	*2.24*	*12*	*0.92*	*5*	*55*

Look For the Good

The song says, "Look for the silver lining in every cloud of gray."

The Good Book says, "All things work together for those that love God." Are we as Christians always looking for the good? Or are we looking to see who did wrong?

There is a story of a couple that had two sons; one was an eternal pessimist, and the other an eternal optimist. The parents took them to a doctor to see if he could bring balance into their lives. The doctor put the pessimist in a room full of all kinds of toys and games for a boy his age.

An hour later, they went into the room only to find the boy standing in the corner. When asked why he hadn't played with anything, the boy answered, "They were probably all broken." The optimist boy was put into a room full of horse manure.

An hour later they found the boy looking all around. When asked what he was doing, he said, "With all this manure around, there must be a pony somewhere." What are we looking for? According to The Good Book, let us look for the good.

GARDEN VEGETABLE SOUP

1 10 3/4-ounce can fat free condensed chicken broth
1 10 3/4-ounce can hot water
1 teaspoon soy sauce
1/8 teaspoon dried thyme leaves
1/8 teaspoon dried basil leaves
1/8 teaspoon onion powder
1/4 pound fresh broccoli, cut into flowerets
1 medium carrot, cut into 2 1/2x1/4-inch strips
1 cup thinly shredded lettuce

METHOD:

In a large saucepan, combine broth, water, soysauce, thyme, basil and onion powder.
Heat to boiling.
Add broccoli and carrots, and cook 4 to 5 minutes until vegetables are tender.
Stir in shredded lettuce.
Serve hot.
Store left over in refrigerator.

SERVES: 4

FAT GRAMS PER SERVING: FAT FREE

Nutritional Analysis Per Serving:

cal	*g. fat*	*(% of cal)*	*g.fib*	*mg. chol*	*mg. sod*
71	*0.41*	*5*	*1.12*	*0.00*	*375*

MACARONI SALAD

1 1/2 cups uncooked macaroni
1 cucumber
2-3 stalks celery
1 tomato
1/2 cup fat free mayonnaise

METHOD:

Cook and cool macaroni.
Chop vegetables and mix with macaroni and mayonnaise.

SERVES: 4

FAT GRAMS PER SERVING: 1

Nutritional Analysis Per Serving:

cal	*g. fat*	*(%of cal)*	*g.fib*	*mg.chol*	*mg. sod*
158	*0.79*	*5*	*2.78*	*0.00*	*399*

ORANGE/CRANBERRY RELISH

1 pound cranberries
1/4 lemon
2 navel oranges
2 cups sugar

METHOD:

Chop cranberries in food processor or blender and set aside.
Cut oranges and lemon into sections and chop in processor.
Add mixtures together and add sugar.
Mix well and chill.

SERVES: 8

FAT GRAMS PER SERVING: FAT FREE

Nutritional Analysis Per Serving:

cal	*g. fat*	*(% of cal)*	*g.fib*	*mg. chol*	*mg. sod*
116	*0.17*	*1*	*2.44*	*0.00*	*1.36*

PERFECTION SALAD

2 tablespoons Knox gelatin
1/2 cup cold water
1/2 cup mild vinegar
2 tablespoons lemon juice
2 cups boiling water
1/2 cup sugar
1 teaspoon salt
1 cup cabbage (finely shredded)
1 2-ounce can pimentos
2 cups celery, cut in small pieces
1/4 cup sweet red or green peppers

METHOD:

Soak gelatine in cold water about 5 minutes.
Add vinegar, lemon juice, boiling water, sugar and salt.
When mixture begins to stiffen, add remaining ingredients.
Turn into wet mold and chill.
Remove to bed of lettuce.
Garnish with fat free mayonnaise dressing.

SERVES: 6

FAT GRAMS PER SERVING: FAT FREE

NOTE: N. analysis does NOT include fat free mayonnaise dressing.

Nutritional Analysis Per Serving:

cal	*g. fat*	*(%of cal)*	*g.fib*	*mg.chol*	*mg. sod*
46	*0.14*	*3*	*1.51*	*0.00*	*198*

POTATO SOUP

4 tablespoons fat free margarine
2 cups skim milk
1/2 cup minced onions
pepper
1/2 cup finely chopped parsley
2 tablespoons flour
4 cups potatoes, diced
3 cups canned fat free beef stock
1 cup fat free sour cream

METHOD:

Melt margarine in kettle and add flour.
Stir in milk.
Add potatoes, onions, stock, and pepper to taste.
Bring to boil and simmer for about 15 minutes.
Puree in processor or blender and return to kettle.
Reheat to near boiling.
Stir in sour cream and parsley.

SERVES: 4

FAT GRAMS PER SERVING: FAT FREE

Nutritional Analysis Per Serving:

cal	*g. fat*	*(% of cal)*	*g.fib*	*mg. chol*	*mg. sod*
321	*0.48*	*1*	*3.10*	*10*	*3457*

Kids?

It is fun to watch kids as they play and become best friends.

Most kids sooner or later will get into some kind of fight. If the parents get involved, look out. The parents get mad at each other for no other reason than to take up for their kids.

In many cases, while the parents are still mad at each other, the kids are back playing together. The lesson most parents eventually learn is to stay out of their kids arguments.

We need to be more like the kids. Most of the time they kiss and make up just about as fast as it started.

They forget quickly because the good of playing together outweighs the bad.

The benefit of walking in love with each other sure outweighs the bad of carrying a hurt or anger. God knows best.

Many times He tells us to look to children. We can learn a lot from our kids if we are open to learn.

PUDDING FRUIT SALAD

1 15-ounce can mandarin oranges, drain and save juice
1 20-ounce can pineapple chunks
3 bananas, cut in large chunks
1 2.9-ounce box sugar free vanilla pudding (cooking kind)
1 to 1 1/2 cups above juice depending on how thick you want glaze

METHOD:

Cook vanilla pudding in the juice until it bubbles and is thick.
Pour hot glaze over fruits and refrigerate.
You can also add peaches, fruit cocktail or apples.

SERVES: 8

FAT GRAMS PER SERVING: 1

Nutritional Analysis Per Serving:

cal	g. fat	(% of cal)	g.fib	mg. chol	mg. sod
154	0.66	4	1.57	0.00	483

RAISIN-CARROT SALAD

1/3 cup seedless raisins
1 cup carrots, finely chopped
1/3 cup finely diced celery
1/2 cup Grape Nuts cereal
1/2 cup fat free mayonnaise
Vanilla extract

METHOD:

Combine raisins, carrots, celery, Grape Nuts cereal.
Add enough mayonnaise to blend, add a few drops of vanilla if desired.
Chill well.
Serve on crisp lettuce leaves.

SERVES: 4

FAT GRAMS PER SERVING: FAT FREE

Nutritional Analysis Per Serving:

cal	*g. fat*	*(%of cal)*	*g.fib*	*mg.chol*	*mg. sod*
165	*0.22*	*1*	*3.65*	*0.00*	*424*

RASPBERRY-PRETZEL SALAD (MICROWAVE)

3/4 cup fat free margarine
1 10-ounce package fat free pretzels crushed (2 cups)
1 3/4 cups hot tap water
6 ounce package raspberry flavored Jello
2 10-ounce packages frozen raspberries
1 8-ounce package fat free cream cheese
2 cups Lite whipped topping
1 1/4 cup sugar

METHOD:

Place margarine in 2-quart utility dish.
Heat on full power for 1 minute 15 seconds to 2 minutes 15 seconds, or until melted. Stir in pretzel crumbs and 1/4 cup sugar.
Press mixture firmly against bottom of dish.
Cook on full power for 1 1/2 to 3 minutes, or until set.
Turn half-turn halfway through cooking time.
Heat water in covered container on full power for 2 to 3 1/2 minutes, or until boiling. Stir in Jello, until dissolved.
Add frozen raspberries. Break apart with fork and stir until berries are separated. Chill until slightly thickened, if necessary.
Cream remaining 1 cup sugar and cream cheese in small mixing bowl, until lite and fluffy.
Fold in whipped topping. Spread over crust and chill.
Spread slightly thickened Jello mixture over cream cheese layer.
Chill until firm.
You may wish to substitute raspberries with strawberries.

SERVES: 12

FAT GRAMS PER SERVING: 1

Nutritional Analysis Per Serving:

cal	*g. fat*	*(% of cal)*	*g.fib*	*mg. chol*	*mg. sod*
184	*1.37*	*7*	*1.88*	*3*	*540*

RICE COLE SLAW

1 quart shredded cabbage
1 cup grated carrots
1/2 cup chopped onion
3 cups cooked rice, cooled
1 tablespoon sugar
1 teaspoon celery seed
1 teaspoon seasoned pepper
1 cup fat free sour cream

METHOD:

Combine the cabbage, carrots, onion and rice in mixing bowl. Blend the remaining ingredients and add to the rice mixture. Toss litely; chill.

SERVES: 16

FAT GRAMS PER SERVING: FAT FREE

Nutritional Analysis Per Serving:

cal	g. fat	(%of cal)	g.fib	mg.chol	mg. sod
77	0.14	2	0.72	2	18

RICE SOUP

2 1/2 cups water
1 tablespoon instant chicken bouillon
2 teaspoons lemon juice
1/4 teaspoons sugar
1/4 cup instant rice
1 6-ounce can tomato paste
1 tablespoon fat free margarine
1/2 teaspoon seasoned salt
1 bay leaf

METHOD:

In pan combine all ingredients.
Bring to a boil.
Cover and remove from heat.
Let stand 7 minutes.
Remove bay leaf.

SERVES: 4

FAT GRAMS PER SERVING: 1

Nutritional Analysis Per Serving:

cal	*g. fat*	*(% of cal)*	*g.fib*	*mg. chol*	*mg. sod*
97	*0.80*	*7*	*3.90*	*0.01*	*293*

SAUSAGE SOUP

1 1/2 pounds Mr. Turkey Sausage
2 cups finely chopped celery
2 52-ounce cans split pea soup
2 teaspoons Worcestershire sauce
2 cups finely chopped onion
2 quarts water
1 quart skim milk

METHOD:

Brown sausage in Nonstick skillet and pour off the drippings.
Cook chopped vegetables in microwave until tender.
Blend in soup and stir in sausage.
Add milk and Worcestershire.
Heat very hot but do not boil.

SERVES: 12

FAT GRAMS PER SERVING: 6

Nutritional Analysis Per Serving:

cal	*g. fat*	*(%of cal)*	*g.fib*	*mg.chol*	*mg. sod*
196	*6.01*	*28*	*3.51*	*37*	*574*

SNACK SALAD

1	head lettuce
1	cup fat free Cheddar cheese, grated
1/2	cup fat free mayonnaise
2	cups chopped apples, unpared
2	tablespoons green onions, sliced
1	tablespoon lemon juice
1/2	cup fat free croutons

METHOD:

Tear lettuce.
Add apples, cheese and green onions.
Combine mayonnaise, lemon juice and salt.
Toss with lettuce mixture.
Add croutons.

SERVES:6

FAT GRAMS PER SERVING: FAT FREE

Nutritional Analysis Per Serving:

cal	*g. fat*	*(% of cal)*	*g.fib*	*mg. chol*	*mg. sod*
143	*0.14*	*1*	*5.13*	*3*	*400*

TEXAS CHILI

1	cup onion, finely chopped
4	tablespoons green pepper, chopped
1	pound lean sirloin
1/2	cup celery, diced
3	tablespoons chili powder
2	teaspoons sugar
1 1/2	cups tomato juice
1	53-ounce can chili beans (optional)

METHOD:

Cook onions and green pepper until tender in sprayed non-stick skillet.
Add meat and cook until brown stirring often.
Drain.
Add remaining ingredients; cook over low heat for several hours. If desired, a large can of chili beans may be added just before serving.

SERVES: 8

FAT GRAMS PER SERVING: 5

Nutritional Analysis Per Serving:

cal	*g. fat*	*(%of cal)*	*g.fib*	*mg.chol*	*mg. sod*
427	*5.03*	*11*	*18.31*	*26*	*1604*

TOMATO SOUP

4	cups cooked carrots
1	green pepper, sliced
3/4	cups vinegar
1	teaspoon dry mustard
1	teaspoon Worcestershire sauce
1	red onion, sliced
1/2	cup water
1	10 1/2-ounce can tomato soup

METHOD:

In bowl combine drained carrots and onions.
Bring remaining ingredients to boil and pour hot mixture over vegetables.
Refrigerate for at least 12 hours.

SERVES: 4

FAT GRAMS PER SERVING: 2

Nutritional Analysis Per Serving:

cal	*g. fat*	*(% of cal)*	*g.fib*	*mg. chol*	*mg. sod*
156	*1.76*	*10*	*5.77*	*0.00*	*649*

TURKEY CHILI

2	pounds ground turkey breast
2	cups chopped onion
2	cloves garlic, crushed
3	tablespoons chili powder
1	teaspoon paprika
1	teaspoon oregano
1	teaspoon ground cumin
1/2	teaspoon cayenne pepper
1/2	cup fat free beef stock
1	3/4 pound fresh tomatoes
3	1-pound cans red kidney beans

METHOD:

In nonstick skillet brown turkey, discarding fat. Combine all ingredients in slow cooker, stirring well. Cook on low 8-10 hours, or on automatic 6 hours. Remember to use your fat free saltine crackers.

SERVES: 10

FAT GRAMS PER SERVING: 2

Nutritional Analysis Per Serving:

cal	*g. fat*	*(%of cal)*	*g.fib*	*mg.chol*	*mg. sod*
293	*1.57*	*5*	*1.90*	*10*	*1445*

Useless

Did you ever play in a game that you were not good at?

When they chose up sides, and you are the last one picked because no one wants you.

Have you ever gone on vacation or been sick and no one missed you? To say that you feel useless would not even begin to cover all the emotions involved. It is an awful feeling to feel unwanted.

The children's story of the "Ugly Duckling" shows some of the hurt, but like most stories, it has a happy ending. Life isn't always that kind. It seems like it never ends.

Well, God has a different set of guide lines. He says that all the parts of the church, the body of Christ, are important.

He says that the eye, the hand, the foot, etc. are all needed. We can't do without anyone. He says that when one hurts, we all hurt.

It doesn't matter if you are picked last, for His Word says that the last will be first and the first last. God cares about everybody.

TURKEY CORN CHOWDER

1	large onion, chopped
1	pound fresh ground turkey breast
1	12-ounce package frozen whole kernel corn
1	large potato, peeled and diced
1	pound fresh tomatoes
1 1/2	teaspoons salt
1/2	teaspoon pepper
2	teaspoons sugar
3	cups boiling water
2/3	cup canned evaporated skim milk

METHOD:

Saute onion in sprayed Nonstick skillet until transparent; push to one side.
Add turkey; cook, stirring until litely browned.
Add remaining ingredients, except milk; stir well.
Cover and bring just to a boil; reduce heat and simmer 30 minutes, or until potatoes are tender.
Just before serving, remove from heat and slowly stir in milk.

SERVES: 8

FAT GRAMS PER SERVING: 1

Nutritional Analysis Per Serving:

cal	g. fat	(%of cal)	g.fib	mg.chol	mg. sod
169	1.07	6	2.36	7	367

VEGETABLE BEAN SOUP

1 pound dry navy beans
6 cups water
1 1/2 sliced carrots
1 28-ounce can tomatoes
1/4 teaspoon pepper
1 pound Mr. Turkey polish sausage
2 medium onions, sliced
2 stalks celery, in chunks
1 teaspoon Worcestershire sauce

METHOD:

Combine all ingredients and simmer covered for 3 to 3 1/2 hours.

SERVES: 10

FAT GRAMS PER SERVING: 2

Nutritional Analysis Per Serving:

cal	*g. fat*	*(% of cal)*	*g.fib*	*mg. chol*	*mg. sod*
271	*2.32*	*8*	*14.16*	*20*	*756*

VEGETABLE SALAD

4 tomatoes
1 cucumber
1 green pepper
1 stalk celery
3 radishes, sliced
1/2 onion, minced
1/4 cabbage, shredded
Salt
Pepper
1/2 cup fat free mayonnaise

METHOD:

Peel and slice tomatoes and cucumbers.
Cut pepper and celery into 1/4-inch pieces.
Mix all ingredients together.
Serve with mayonnaise in bowl lined with lettuce.

SERVES: 8

FAT GRAMS PER SERVING: 1

Nutritional Analysis Per Serving:

cal	g. fat	(%of cal)	g.fib	mg.chol	mg. sod
60	0.51	8	1.94	0.00	158

VEGETABLE SOUP

1 pound ground turkey breast
1/2 cup chopped onion
2 quarts water
2 beef bouillon cubes
1 cup diced celery
1 cup diced carrots
1 cup diced potatoes
2 cups shredded cabbage
1 (No. 2) can tomatoes or
1 46-ounce can V-8 juice

METHOD:

Brown meat in sprayed nonstick skillet.
Add all ingredients in large pan.
Simmer 2-3 hours.

SERVES: 8

FAT GRAMS PER SERVING: 1

Nutritional Analysis Per Serving:

cal	*g. fat*	*(% of cal)*	*g.fib*	*mg. chol*	*mg. sod*
71	*0.54*	*7*	*2.50*	*6*	*276*

WESTERN CHILI CON CARNE

2 cups dry pinto beans
6 cups water
1 cup chopped onion
2 cloves garlic, minced
1 1/2 pounds lean ground sirloin
4-6 teaspoons chili powder
2 teaspoons paprika
1 teaspoon dried oregano, crushed
1/2 teaspoon pepper
1/4 teaspoon ground cumin
2 bay leaves
1 28-ounce can tomatoes, undrained
3 tablespoons yellow cornmeal
Dash of cayenne (optional)
Baked fat free flour tortillas (optional)

Cont'd on next page

WESTERN CONT'D

METHOD:

Wash beans; soak in water overnight.
(Or, for quick-soak method, bring beans and hot water to a boil; boil 2 minutes.
Remove from heat, cover and let stand 1 hour.)
Simmer soaked beans about 1 1/2 hours, or until tender; drain, reserving 1 cup liquid.
Meanwhile, saute onion and garlic in sprayed nonstick skillet until tender, but not brown.
Add beef; brown, breaking apart with a fork.
Stir in beans, reserved liquid, chili powder, paprika, salt, oregano, pepper, cumin, bay leaves and tomatoes; bring to a boil. Reduce heat and simmer over low heat, uncovered, about 1 1/2 hours, stirring occasionally. To thicken, add cornmeal slowly, stirring constantly; cook over medium-high heat until chili boils. Taste; add cayenne if desired. For maximum flavor, cover and refrigerate overnight; reheat before serving. Serve with flour tortillas if desired.

SERVES: 10

FAT GRAMS PER SERVING: 3

Nutritional Analysis Per Serving:

cal	*g. fat*	*(% of cal)*	*g.fib*	*mg. chol*	*mg. sod*
195	*3.05*	*14*	*4.14*	*31*	*337*

Got a Problem?

Paul had a problem called, "A thorn in the flesh."

Different people have different views as to what the thorn was, but there is no question as to God's answer: "My grace is sufficient." Paul went to God three times and God said, "My grace is sufficient."

God says when you are weak and can't handle the problem, that is when He (God) can show His strength.

God just wants us to cast our cares on Him so He can work them out. Moses had a problem when they came to the Red Sea and the army was behind them.

The bigger the problems, the more God has a chance to be God in the situation. It is His grace, His power, and His Will being done on earth as it is in Heaven. God then gets the glory, which is a testimony to those who see it.

Your problem gets taken care of, God gets the glory, and some may come to know Him because of your testimony.

VEGGIES

INDEX TO VEGGIES

BROCCOLI AND CORN BAKE

1 10-ounce box frozen broccoli, thawed and drained
1/4 cup fat free cracker crumbs
1 ounce fat free egg substitute
1 15-ounce can cream style corn
2 tablespoons fat free margarine
1 tablespoon minced onion (dry)
1/2 teaspoon salt
Dash of pepper

METHOD:

Mix together and bake in casserole dish.
Top with cracker crumbs before baking at 350 degrees for 35 to 40 minutes.

SERVES: 8

FAT GRAMS PER SERVING: 1

Nutritional Analysis Per Serving:

cal	*g. fat*	*(% of cal)*	*g.fib*	*mg. chol*	*mg. sod*
154	*1.02*	*6*	*1.67*	*0.25*	*113*

Old Times

What are the good old times? Back when movies were twenty-five cents and popcorn ten cents? Gas was twenty-five cents a gallon? Minimum wage was one dollar and fifteen cents?

Maybe it was before air travel, the automobile, TV, electric lights and so on. Jesus said that once you put your hand to the plow, you shouldn't look back.

The reason is, that if you keep looking back, you can't plow a straight line. You need to keep your focus on where you are going.

The Good Book says, "For whatever was written in earlier times was written for our instruction, that through perserverance and the encouragement of the Scripture, we might have hope." It is the hope or expectancy, that what God did before, He will do again. God's Word says, "He does not change." That is our hope and faith. If He did it for them, He will do it for us. These are the old times that are good to hope for, and believe in, and focus on.

BROCCOLI AND RICE DELUXE (MICROWAVE RECIPE)

1 tablespoon fat free margarine
1/2 cup chopped onion
1 1/2 cups quick cooking rice
1 1/2 cups hot tap water
1 10-ounce package frozen chopped broccoli or spinach
5 ounces fat free block cheese
1 10 3/4-ounce can cream of mushroom soup
1/8 teaspoon nutmeg (optional)

Method:
Combine margarine and onion in 1 1/2-quart casserole dish.
Cook, covered, on full power for 2 1/2 to 4 minutes, or until onion is tender.
Add rice and water.
Cook, covered, on full power for 4 to 6 minutes, or until boiling.
Let stand, covered, until moisture is absorbed.
Place frozen broccoli in 1-quart casserole dish.
Cook, covered, on full power for 4 to 6 minutes, or until tender. Stir halfway through cooking time to break apart.
Drain.
Stir broccoli, cheese and soup into rice mixture.
Add nutmeg, if desired.
Heat on full power for 4 1/2 to 6 1/2 minutes, or until heated through.

SERVES: 6

FAT GRAMS PER SERVING: 4

Nutritional Analysis Per Serving:

cal	*g. fat*	*(% of cal)*	*g.fib*	*mg. chol*	*mg. sod*
204	*4.25*	*19*	*1.71*	*4*	*776*

BROCCOLI PIE

2 10-ounce packages frozen, chopped broccoli
3 cups shredded fat free Cheddar cheese
2/3 cup chopped onion
1 1/3 cups skim milk
6 ounces fat free egg substitute
3/4 cup Lite Bisquick
1/4 teaspoon pepper

METHOD:

Heat oven to 400 degrees.
Grease pie plate, 10x1 1/2 inches.
Rinse broccoli under running cold water to thaw; drain thoroughly.
Mix broccoli, 2 cups of the cheese and onion in plate.
Beat fat free egg substitute, milk, baking mix, and pepper until smooth, 1 minute with hand beater.
Pour into plate.
Bake until knife inserted in the center comes out clean, 25-35 minutes.
Top with the remaining cheese.
Bake until cheese melts, 1-2 minutes; cool 5 minutes.

SERVES: 8

FAT GRAMS PER SERVING: 1

Nutritional Analysis Per Serving:

cal	*g. fat*	*(%of cal)*	*g.fib*	*mg.chol*	*mg. sod*
177	*1.22*	*6*	*1.65*	*7*	*542*

Mondays

Unless you are really a "Gun Ho," a Self-Starter, a really Motivated-Type person, Mondays are not generally the best day of the week.

If it wasn't for the fact that we might lose our jobs or flunk out of school, many people would like to start their work week on Tuesday. It is the fear of some type of punishment that gets most people going on Monday.

The leaders can't wait for the weekend to get over so that they can get going. If we were all leaders we would have no workers, and it takes more workers to get the job done. What does this have to do with Christianity?

Well, since most of us fall into the worker category, we need some motivation to get us going. What God has given to us today is by His grace and mercy. God has given us the free will to do what we want.

That makes it hard for us to get started as to our praying or reading the Bible.The Good Book says to "Enter His gates with thanksgiving and into His courts with praise." That isn't too hard to do, then everything else will fall into place.

EXERCISE

For several years, Americans have been pursuing exercise as never before. Those who have been studied as to the effect of exercise report more efficient hearts, improved endurance, ability to do more work easier, and less stress and tension.

One specialist in the health field has said, "If we could find a cure for cancer right now, it might increase the average life span by two years. But if we bring every man, woman and child down to his proper weight, it could increase the life span by seven years."

However, all exercise is not helpful. I read about a new plan that is guaranteed to burn up a certain number of calories per hours. I would not endorse it, but you just might want to take a look at it:

Beating around the bush .... 75 calories
Jumping to conclusion .... 100 calories
Passing the buck .... 25 calories
Throwing your weight around .... 399 calories
Dragging your heels .... 100 calories
Sidestepping responsibility .... 25 calories
Pushing your luck .... 150 calories

The exercise of the body has value, but godliness is more important.

Another exercise recommended in The Good Book is that of good judgment.
Author Unknown

CAJUN GREEN BEANS

2 15 1/2-ounce cans green beans
4 pieces turkey bacon
1 small onion, chopped
1/2 teaspoon garlic powder
Black pepper to taste

METHOD:

Cut bacon into small pieces and cook in 3-quart sauce pan until done.
Add onion, cook until limp.
Add beans, garlic and black pepper.
Cook until almost dry.

SERVES: 8

FAT GRAMS PER SERVING: 1

Nutritional Analysis Per Serving:

cal	*g. fat*	*(% of cal)*	*g.fib*	*mg. chol*	*mg. sod*
40	*1.39*	*31*	*1.26*	*5*	*503*

FAMILY

A family is a **PLACE** - to cry and laugh, and vent frustrations, to ask for help, and tease and yell, to be touched and hugged and smiled at.

A family is **PEOPLE** - who care when you are sad, who love you no matter what, who share your triumphs, who don't expect you to be perfect, just growing with honesty in your own direction.

A family is a **CIRCLE** - where we learn to like ourselves, where we learn to make good decisions, where we learn to think before we do, where we learn integrity and respect for other people, where we are special, where we learn the rules of life.

The world is **PLACE** - where anything can happen. If we grow up in a loving family, we are ready for the world.

Author Unknown

CARROT SOUFFLE WITH CHEESE

1 cup cooked, mashed carrots
4 ounces fat free egg substitute
1/2 cup rolled fat free cracker crumbs
1 cup skim milk
1/2 teaspoon pepper
1 tablespoon sugar
6 tablespoons melted fat free margarine
1 cup fat free grated cheese

METHOD:

Mix all ingredients together and bake 45 minutes at 375 degrees.

SERVES: 4

FAT GRAMS PER SERVING: 1

Nutritional Analysis Per Serving:

cal	*g. fat*	*(% of cal)*	*g.fib*	*mg. chol*	*mg. sod*
309	*0.90*	*3*	*4.52*	*6*	*620*

CAULIFLOWER ORIENTAL MICROWAVE RECIPE

1 medium head cauliflower, broken into pieces
2 tablespoons water
1/2 onion, chopped
1/2 cup diced celery
1 tablespoon chopped parsley
1 tablespoon fat free margarine
1 cup hot tap water
1 teaspoon instant chicken flavored bouillon
1 tablespoon cornstarch
1 tablespoon soy sauce
Dash pepper

Cont'd on next page

CAULIFLOWER ORIENTAL CONT'D

METHOD:

Combine cauliflower and water in 2-quart casserole dish.
Cook, covered, on full power for 6 to 9 minutes, or until tender. Let stand, covered.
Combine onion, celery, parsley and margarine in 1-quart casserole.
Cook, covered, on full power for 3 to 5 minutes, or until vegetables are tender. Stir halfway through cooking time.
Place water in 2-quart glass measuring cup.
Heat on full power for 1 1/2 to 2 1/2 minutes, or until boiling.
Dissolve bouillon cube in water. Blend in cornstarch, soy sauce and pepper.
Pour sauce over onion mixture.
Cook, covered, on full power for 3 to 5 minutes or until thickened.
Stir halfway through cooking time. Drain cauliflower.
Return to casserole. Pour sauce over cauliflower. Mix thoroughly.
Heat on full power for 3 to 5 minutes, or until heated through. Two (10 ounce each) packages frozen cauliflower may be used instead of fresh.

SERVES: 6

FAT GRAMS PER SERVING: 1

Nutritional Analysis Per Serving:

cal	*g. fat*	*(% of cal)*	*g.fib*	*mg. chol*	*mg. sod*
83	*0.55*	*6*	*7.59*	*0.00*	*583*

CHEESE-SCALLOPED CARROTS (MICROWAVE RECIPE)

4 cups sliced carrots
1 tablespoon water
1/4 cup minced onion
2 tablespoons fat free margarine
2 tablespoons all-purpose flour
1/4 teaspoon dry mustard
1/4 teaspoon celery salt
Dash pepper
1 cup skim milk
1/4 pound shredded fat free Cheddar cheese
1/2 cup fat free cracker crumbs

METHOD:

Combine carrots and water in 1 1/2-quart casserole dish.
Cook, covered, on full power for 9 to 12 minutes, or until crisp-tender.
Drain and remove carrots. Set aside.
Place onion and margarine in 1 1/2-quart casserole dish.
Cook, covered, on full power for 1 1/2 to 3 minutes, or until tender.
Blend in flour, mustard, salt and pepper. Slowly stir in milk.
Cook, covered, on full power for 3 1/2 to 5 1/2 minutes, or until thickened.
Stir several times during cooking time. Stir in cheese until melted.
Mix in carrots.
Top with cracker crumbs.
Heat on full power for 3 1/2 to 5 1/2 minutes, or until heated through.

SERVES: 8

FAT GRAMS PER SERVING: FAT FREE

Nutritional Analysis Per Serving:

cal	*g. fat*	*(%of cal)*	*g.fib*	*mg.chol*	*mg. sod*
159	*0.20*	*1*	*2.04*	*9*	*541*

CORN & RICE

2 15-ounce cans cream corn
1 cup Minute Rice
4 ounces fat free egg substitute
1 tablespoon sugar
8 ounces fat free margarine
1 onion, chopped
1 2-ounce can pimentos
1 bell pepper, chopped
3/4 cup shredded fat free cheddar cheese

METHOD:

Saute onion and bell pepper in margarine.
Add all ingredients together in baking dish.
Shredded fat free cheese over top.
Bake 30 minutes at 350 degrees.
SERVES: 8

FAT GRAMS PER SERVING: FAT FREE

Nutritional Analysis Per Serving:

cal	*g. fat*	*(% of cal)*	*g.fib*	*mg. chol*	*mg. sod*
248	*0.10*	*1*	*2.63*	*2*	*772*

Fifty Percent

In the advertising profession, the chairman of one of the largest agencies in the world once said, "We know that fifty percent of the advertising we do is wasted; the only problem is, we aren't sure which fifty percent."

We know that our tax money is wasted in many areas but it is hard to get any real agreement in government as to where it is.

There is wasted money, time and effort in most business, schools and even in the home.

You may feel that way in what you do for the Lord. Sometimes you feel like you have wasted your time in helping someone or sharing Jesus with someone. Well, in God's kingdom things aren't wasted.

The Good Book says that God's Word will not return to Him empty, without accomplishing that which is pleasing to Him, and without succeeding in the matter for which He sent it. Jesus said that if you give a drink to a little one, you won't lose your reward. What you do for God is never wasted.

CORN FAIRFAX

2 14 1/2-ounce cans whole green beans
8 ounces fat free margarine
2 15-ounce cans whole green asparagus
8 ounces fat free egg substitute
2 pounds frozen cream style corn
1 cup evaporated skim milk
1 onion, chopped
1 bell pepper, chopped
1 cup diced celery
1 cup crushed corn flakes

METHOD:

Saute onions, peppers and celery until tender in margarine. Mix with beaten fat free egg substitute, salt, evaporated milk and corn. Drain beans and place in sprayed casserole dish. Place drained asparagus on top of beans.
Pour corn mixture over all and sprinkle crushed corn flakes on top.
Bake in slow oven, 275 degrees for 1 hour.

SERVES: 20

FAT GRAMS PER SERVING: 2

Nutritional Analysis Per Serving:

cal	*g. fat*	*(% of cal)*	*g.fib*	*mg. chol*	*mg. sod*
140	*1.75*	*11*	*4.03*	*0.46*	*596*

COWBOY BEANS

1 1/2 cups pinto beans
6 slices turkey bacon
1 small onion
1/2 cup catsup
2 tablespoons molasses
1/4 teaspoon pepper
1/2 teaspoon dry mustard
1 teaspoon Worcestershire sauce

METHOD:

Wash and drain beans.
Soak beans overnight in fresh water (using about 4 1/2 cups).
Place beans in slow cooker in soaking water.
Cook on high for 3 hours.
Add other ingredients to slow cooker.
Cook on low 12-14 hours, or until tender.

SERVES: 6

FAT GRAMS PER SERVING: 3

Nutritional Analysis Per Serving:

cal	*g. fat*	*(%of cal)*	*g.fib*	*mg.chol*	*mg. sod*
235	*3.05*	*12*	*3.87*	*10*	*961*

CREAMED ASPARAGUS

1 15-ounce can asparagus
1/2 10 3/4-ounce can cream of mushroom soup
2 ounces fat free margarine
1/2 12-ounce can evaporated skim milk
2 hard-cooked egg whites
1/2 cup fat free cracker crumbs
8 ounce package fat free grated cheese

METHOD:

Heat together mushroom soup, milk and margarine.
Add chopped hard-cooked egg whites.
In a small baking dish, put layer of cracker crumbs, layer of asparagus, then soup mixture.
Continue with layers of each and top with cracker crumbs and grated cheese.
Bake at 350 degrees until hot through and through.

SERVES: 4

FAT GRAMS PER SERVING: 5

Nutritional Analysis Per Serving:

cal	*g. fat*	*(% of cal)*	*g.fib*	*mg. chol*	*mg. sod*
546	*5.50*	*9*	*6.84*	*34*	*3135*

CREAMED CAULIFLOWER MICROWAVE RECIPE

1 head cauliflower
2 tablespoons fat free margarine
2 tablespoons flour
1 1/2 cups skim milk
1/2 teaspoon salt
1/4 teaspoon pepper
2 tablespoons chopped pimento (optional)
1/2 cup green onions, chopped (optional)
1/4 cup fat free bread crumbs, spread with Fat free margarine
1/2 cup fat free grated cheese

METHOD:

Cook the cauliflower in boiling, salted water for about 20 minutes. Drain.
Break cauliflower into florets and place in baking dish.
Melt margarine in small pot.
Add flour and stir until blended.
Gradually add milk, stirring until smooth and thick.
Add salt, pepper, pimento and green onions.
Blend well.
Pour over florets.
Sprinkle with grated cheese and bread crumbs.
Bake in 375 degree oven for 20 minutes or until slightly browned.

SERVES: 8

FAT GRAMS PER SERVING: FAT FREE

Nutritional Analysis Per Serving:

cal	g. fat	(%of cal)	g.fib	mg.chol	mg. sod
100	0.48	4	5.79	2	206

CREAMY BROCCOLI BAKE

1 1/2 pounds broccoli or 1 medium head cauliflower,
separated into floweretes
1/2 10 1/2-ounce can cream of mushroom soup
1/2 cup skim milk
1/2 cup shredded fat free Cheddar cheese (about 2 ounce)
1 cup Bisquick baking mix
1/4 cup fat free margarine

METHOD:

Heat 1 cup of water ; add broccoli.
Cover and heat to boiling.
Cook until stems are almost tender, 10 to 12 minutes; drain.
Place broccoli in ungreased 1 1/2-quart round casserole dish.
Heat oven to 400 degrees.
Beat soup and milk with hand beater until smooth; pour over broccoli.
Sprinkle with cheese.
Mix baking mix and margarine until crumbly; sprinkle over cheese. Bake until crumbs are lite brown, about 20 minutes.
Two (10 ounce) packages frozen broccoli spears or cauliflower, cooked and drained, can be substituted.

SERVES: 6

FAT GRAMS PER SERVING: 4

Nutritional Analysis Per Serving:

cal	*g. fat*	*(% of cal)*	*g.fib*	*mg. chol*	*mg. sod*
158	*3.58*	*20*	*3.84*	*2*	*610*

CREOLE CAULIFLOWER AU GRATIN

4 tablespoons fat free margarine
1 onion, chopped
1/2 green pepper, chopped
2 tablespoons flour
2 cups cooked tomatoes, mashed
1 teaspoon salt
1/2 teaspoon peppper
3 cups cooked cauliflower
1/2 cup fat free grated cheese

METHOD:

Melt margarine in a saucepan, add onion and pepper and brown litely.
Blend in flour, add tomatoes and salt.
Heat to boiling point and cook 3 minutes, stirring constantly.
Add cauliflower and heat thoroughly.
Place mixture in a casserole and cover with 1/2 cup grated cheese.
Bake in 350 degree oven until cheese has melted and mixture is hot and bubbly.

SERVES: 6

FAT GRAMS PER SERVING: 1

Nutritional Analysis Per Serving:

cal	*g. fat*	*(%of cal)*	*g.fib*	*mg.chol*	*mg. sod*
94	*0.62*	*6*	*4.14*	*1*	*280*

CREOLE OKRA

3/4 cup sliced okra
2 tablespoons minced onion
2 tablespoons minced green pepper
1 tablespoon fat free margarine
3/4 cup chopped tomatoes
1 teaspoon sugar
1/4 teaspoon salt
1/4 teaspoon black pepper

METHOD:

Saute okra, onion and green pepper in margarine 5 minutes stirring constantly.
Stir in remaining ingredients.
Cook over low heat 10 to 15 minutes, stirring occasionally.

SERVES: 2

FAT GRAMS PER SERVING: FAT FREE

Nutritional Analysis Per Serving:

cal	*g. fat*	*(% of cal)*	*g.fib*	*mg. chol*	*mg. sod*
43	*0.29*	*6*	*1.87*	*0.00*	*292*

Cash A Check

Have you cashed a check lately? It is hard to go very long without writing or cashing a check today.

The important part about it all, is there money in the bank to cover the check?

Some people do write bad checks once in a while by mistake and some are on purpose without having the money in the bank. It is called being overdrawn. The bank doesn't like it and charges you for doing it. Do it too often and you can get into trouble.

God has given us a checking account with Him. Not like a "Sugar Daddy," but He has told us that there is enough to cover all our needs.

With any task that He asks us to do.

The Good Book says that He has already given us everything that we need for life and godliness through the true knowledge of Him who called us.

It is then up to us to draw on our account with God with the same faith that we have when we write a check knowing that the money is in the bank.

EASY THREE-BEAN BAKE

SAUCE:

1 cup chopped onion
1 cup catsup
1/4 cup lite brown sugar
1/2 teaspoon dry mustard

BEANS:

1 10-ounce package frozen lima beans
3 1-pound cans pork and beans
2 15.5-ounce cans kidney beans, drained

METHOD:

In Nonstick skillet saute onion until golden brown, 5 minutes. Add catsup, brown sugar, salt and mustard.
Bring to a boil; reduce heat and simmer, uncovered, 5 minutes. Cook lima beans as directed; drain.
In large bowl, combine sauce, lima beans, pork and beans and kidney beans; mix well.
Turn into 4-quart baking dish.
Bake, uncovered, 40 minutes, or until bubbly (preheat oven to 375 degrees).

SERVES: 12

FAT GRAMS PER SERVING: 4

Nutritional Analysis Per Serving:

cal	g. fat	(% of cal)	g.fib	mg. chol	mg. sod
478	4.41	8	24.01	16	2175

Depressed?

Do you feel like depression is coming down on you?

What have you been listening to lately? The Good Book tells us that faith comes by hearing. Well, so does depression.

You can listen to some sad music. You can listen to some good music that can bring back sad memories. It doesn't have to be music.

People can start talking about sad things. The news and stock market reports can get you depressed. Even ball games can get you down when your favorite team or person doesn't win. There are movies and TV shows that can pull you down.

These are all things that we have control over. If you know that they bother you, don't listen.

We need to keep our shield of faith up at all times. The Good Book says that we are in a battle and we need to be taking every thought captive to the obedience of Christ. If some of these things bother us, we need to be in control and say, "I won't listen, watch or read that."

GARDENER'S VEGETABLE PIE

CRUST:

4 medium potatoes
4 ounces fat free egg substitute
1/2 cup fat free sour cream
1/4 cup grated fat free Parmesan cheese
1/4 teaspoon salt
1/4 teaspoon pepper

FILLING:

2 cups sliced zucchini
1/4 cup sliced green onion
1 cup halved fresh mushrooms
1 1/2 cups chopped tomatoes
1 teaspoon Italian seasoning
1/2 teaspoon salt
1/2 teaspoon garlic powder
1/8 teaspoon pepper

TOPPING:

1 1/2 cups shredded fat free Cheddar cheese

GARDENER'S VEGETABLE PIE CONT'D

METHOD:

Pierce potatoes and arrange on microwave-safe paper towel in oven.
Cook on full power for 10 to 14 minutes, or until done.
Turn potatoes over halfway through cooking time.
Let stand until cool enough to handle.
Peel potatoes and place in mixing bowl.
Mash potatoes.
Set aside.
Combine zucchini, green onion, mushrooms and tomatoes in 2-quart casserole dish.
Cook, covered, on full power for 8 to 10 minutes, or until all are tender.
Stir halfway through cooking time.
Drain well.
Add seasonings.
Place potato mixture in 9-inch pie plate and form into crust.
Spoon cooked vegetables into crust.
Heat on full power for 4 to 5 minutes, or until heated through.
Sprinkle shredded Cheddar cheese over top.
Let stand for 5 minutes to melt cheese.

SERVES: 8

FAT GRAMS PER SERVING: FAT FREE

Nutritional Analysis Per Serving:

cal	*g. fat*	*(%of cal)*	*g.fib*	*mg.chol*	*mg. sod*
149	*0.29*	*2*	*1.88*	*5*	*326*

Pizza?

How do you like your pizza-thick, thin, extra crispy, deep dish, plain or with everything?

There are as many ways to fix pizza today as there are companies that make them, not to mention the ones made at home.

Everyone has their own favorite, which is why we have so many different kinds. Our religion has gotten that way today.

We have gotten so many today that it is hard to keep track. If you can't find one you like, just start your own.

When we get to heaven we will all come together in unity, worshipping God together. Heaven won't be sectioned off by church names.

If there is a sign it may just say, "The Bride of Christ." We don't know a lot about Heaven, but whatever goes on, we will enjoy it, or it wouldn't be Heaven.

LEMON BASIL CARROTS

1 pound baby carrots or medium carrots, cut in 2 1/2-inch pieces
2 tablespoons fat free margarine
1 tablespoon lemon juice
1/2 teaspoon garlic salt
1/2 teaspoon dried basil, crunched
Dash of pepper

METHOD:

In saucepan cook carrots in boiling water for 20 to 30 minutes or until tender; drain.
In saucepan melt margarine, stir in lemon juice, garlic, salt, basil and then add carrots.
Toss.

SERVES: 6

FAT GRAMS PER SERVING: FAT FREE

Nutritional Analysis Per Serving:

cal	*g. fat*	*(%of cal)*	*g.fib*	*mg.chol*	*mg. sod*
68	*0.30*	*4*	*4.61*	*0.00*	*203*

MUSHROOM SOUFFLE

1 pound mushrooms, diced
1/2 cup fat free margarine, melted
10 slices fat free white bread
1/2 cup onion, finely chopped
1/2 cup celery, finely chopped
1/2 cup green pepper, finely chopped
1/2 cup fat free mayonnaise
8 ounces fat free egg substitute
1 1/2 cups skim milk
1/4 teaspoon pepper
1 10 1/2-ounce can cream of mushroom soup
1 cup grated fat free Cheddar cheese

METHOD:

Saute mushrooms in margarine; reserve.
Butter white bread with fat free margarine and cut into 1-inch cubes.
Put half of the bread in shallow 2-quart baking dish.
Combine mushrooms and the remaining ingredients, except soup and cheese.
Spoon over bread.
Top with half of the remaining bread.
Refrigerate overnight.
Before baking, spread soup over all.
Top with remaining bread and bake at 300 degrees for 40 minutes. Sprinkle 1/2 pound grated fat free American cheese.

MUSHROOM SOUFFLE CONT'D

METHOD:

Cook spinach and noodles separately in boiling salted water. Drain and chop fine.
Into well-sprayed ring mold, alternate sections of spinach and noodles, placing small amount of cheese between.
Mix beaten egg substitute with milk and pour over mixture.
Top with bread crumbs, cheese and pieces of margarine.
Bake about 15 minutes at 350 degrees.

SERVES: 8

FAT GRAMS PER SERVING: 3

Nutritional Analysis Per Serving:

cal	*g. fat*	*(%of cal)*	*g.fib*	*mg.chol*	*mg. sod*
195	*3.10*	*14*	*3.45*	*3*	*857*

NOODLE RING WITH SPINACH

2 pounds or 1 package frozen spinach
6 ounces yokeless noodles
4 ounces fat free egg substitute
1/2 cup skim milk
1/2 pound grated fat free American cheese
5 slices Fat free bread crumbs
2 ounces Fat free margarine

METHOD:

Cook spinach and noodles separately in boiling salted water. Drain and chop fine. Into well-sprayed ring mold, alternate sections of spinach and noodles, placing small amount of cheese between. Mix beaten egg substitute with milk and pour over mixture. Top with bread crumbs, cheese and pieces of margarine. Bake about 15 minutes at 350 degrees.

SERVES: 8

FAT GRAMS PER SERVING: 1

Nutritional Analysis Per Serving:

cal	*g. fat*	*(% of cal)*	*g.fib*	*mg. chol*	*mg. sod*
267	*0.75*	*3*	*6.93*	*4*	*559*

WALKING WITH GRANDMA

I like to walk with Grandma,
Her steps are short like mine.
She doesn't say "Now hurry up,"
She always takes her time.

I like to walk with Grandma,
Her eyes see things like mine do...
Wee pebbles bright,
a funny cloud,
Half-hidden drops of dew.

Most people have to hurry,
They do not stop and see...
I'm glad that God made Grandma.
Unrushed and young like me!
Author Unknown

PIMENTO LIMA BEANS

1 15-ounce package frozen limas
2 tablespoons chopped pimento
2 tablespoons chives
1/2 teaspoon salt
1/2 teaspoon garlic salt
1/2 cup fat free sour cream

METHOD:

Boil limas as per package directions; drain excess water, add all above ingredients, then toss with just enough sour cream to coat beans.
Place in casserole dish and keep warm until serving time.

SERVES: 4

FAT GRAMS PER SERVING: FAT FREE

Nutritional Analysis Per Serving:

cal	*g. fat*	*(% of cal)*	*g.fib*	*mg. chol*	*mg. sod*
177	*0.47*	*2*	*4.52*	*4*	*358*

Quotes for the Day

When you aim for perfection you discover it's moving target.

--george fisher

For peace of mind, resign as general manager of the universe.

--larry eisenberg

The worst prison would be a closed heart.

--Pope John Paul II

SLICED BAKED POTATOES

4 medium even potatoes
1 teaspoon salt
3 tablespoons melted fat free margarine
4 tablespoons grated fat free Cheddar cheese
1 1/2 tablespoons fat free Parmesan cheese

METHOD:

Peel potatoes if the skin is tough, otherwise just scrub and rinse them.
Cut potatoes into thin slices but not all the way through.
Use a handle of a spoon to prevent knife from cutting all the way.
Put potatoes in a baking dish.
Fan them slightly.
Sprinkle with salt and drizzle with margarine.
Bake potatoes at 425 degrees for about 50 minutes or until done.
Remove from oven.
Sprinkle with cheese.
Bake potatoes for another 10 to 15 minutes until litely browned, cheeses are melted and potatoes are soft inside.
Check with a fork.

SERVES: 4

FAT GRAMS PER SERVING: FAT FREE

Suggest herbs such as chopped parsley, chives, thyme, or sage.
N. analysis does NOT include herbs.

Nutritional Analysis Per Serving:

cal	*g. fat*	*(% of cal)*	*g.fib*	*mg. chol*	*mg. sod*
150	*0.16*	*1*	*2.55*	*1*	*362*

Attitude?

Has anyone ever told you that you don't look good?

Have they made negative comments about your clothes or hair style? People can hurt you by the things that they say unknowingly. It can ruin your whole day.

Someone may cut you off on the highway, take your parking place, or call you a liar. If you take any one thing personal, it can steal your joy and allow anger to fester in your mind.

Your whole attitude can be controlled by how you handle every situation. Does the situation control you and rob your joy, or do you control it?

Nothing has actually changed other than the way you decide to handle it. The other person may be having a great day. You should too. We need to take control of those fiery darts (thoughts) and refuse to accept them. No matter what people do or say to you, you need to keep your thoughts on who you are in Jesus and what He has done for you.

SOUTH OF THE BORDER LIMAS

1 pound dried lima beans
1/2 cup minced onion
1 green pepper, cut into strips
1 clove garlic, minced
1 tablespoon dill weed
1 pound fresh tomatoes
1 4-ounce can tomato sauce

METHOD:

Soak beans overnight in water.
Drain beans.
Place in cooker with all other ingredients.
Cook on high 3 hours, then switch to low 6 hours.
Or cook on automatic 5-6 hours.

SERVES: 6

FAT GRAMS PER SERVING: 1

Nutritional Analysis Per Serving:

cal	*g. fat*	*(% of cal)*	*g.fib*	*mg. chol*	*mg. sod*
137	*1.15*	*8*	*5.23*	*0.00*	*492*

SPINACH SOUFFLE

2 tablespoons fat free margarine
2 tablespoons flour
1/2 teaspoon pepper
1/2 cup skim milk
1 cup grated fat free Cheddar cheese
1/2 teaspoon Worcestershire sauce
1 cup pureed spinach
12 ounces fat free egg substitute

METHOD:

Make a thick white sauce with margarine, flour, milk and seasoning; add the cheese and Worcestershire sauce and stir over a low heat until cheese melts.
Stir in the spinach and mix thoroughly.
Add fat free egg substitute.
Turn into a well-sprayed casserole dish and bake in a moderately hot oven, 400 degrees for 30 minutes.

SERVES: 4

FAT GRAMS PER SERVING: FAT FREE

Nutritional Analysis Per Serving:

cal	*g. fat*	*(%of cal)*	*g.fib*	*mg.chol*	*mg. sod*
123	*0.19*	*1*	*1.55*	*5*	*449*

SPEEDY BAKED BEANS

4 strips turkey bacon, diced
1 large onion, minced
2 cans pork and beans (No. 1 Tall)
1/4 cup chili sauce
1 teaspoon prepared mustard

METHOD:

Saute turkey bacon until crisp and onion is yellow. Stir in other ingredients. Pour into casserole dish. Bake uncovered until beans are brown and bubbly. Serve hot. Bake at 350 degrees for 45 minutes.

SERVES: 8

FAT GRAMS PER SERVING: 5

Nutritional Analysis Per Serving:

cal	*g. fat*	*(% of cal)*	*g.fib*	*mg. chol*	*mg. sod*
270	*4.78*	*16*	*12.75*	*21*	*1135*

SPINACH TREAT

1/2 pound fat free cottage cheese (small curd)
4 ounces fat free margarine
3 tablespoons flour
6 ounces fat free egg substitute
10 ounce package frozen spinach
6 slices fat free sharp cheese

METHOD:

Mix all together, reserving some cheese for topping. Bake in sprayed 8x8-inch pan or dish for 1 hour at 350 degrees.

SERVES: 6

FAT GRAMS PER SERVING: FAT FREE

Nutritional Analysis Per Serving:

cal	*g. fat*	*(%of cal)*	*g.fib*	*mg.chol*	*mg. sod*
272	*0.19*	*1*	*1.53*	*19*	*1324*

SQUASH SUPREME

4 cups yellow squash, (3 pounds) cooked and diced
1 1/2 cups water
2 tablespoons grated onion
1/4 cup grated carrots
1 10 1/2-ounce can cream of chicken soup
1 cup fat free sour cream
Dash of pepper
2 cups herb seasoned stuffing
3 tablespoons fat free margarine

METHOD:

Mix all together.
Bake at 350 degrees until heated through.

SERVES: 8

FAT GRAMS PER SERVING: 3

Nutritional Analysis Per Serving:

cal	*g. fat*	*(% of cal)*	*g.fib*	*mg. chol*	*mg. sod*
214	*3.03*	*13*	*2.72*	*7*	*518*

My Job

Before long, our job can become our god. We look to the job for security, the money that we need, the medical care, the self-satisfaction and fulfillment.

It becomes our source of support for all of our needs. After awhile, it can even take over the value of your own abilities and you can even doubt in yourself, which makes the job the number-one god. Not because of any great move nor circumstances, I have learned that my job was not my source.

The Good Book says it over and over, that He is our source, but this is a real world and those that don't help themselves don't get help.

I am not saying that you shouldn't work but our trust and faith must be in God. When it is, if something happens to that all-important job, it isn't the end of the world.

He is our source for all our needs. If God could, and did, provide for all those thousands of people in the wilderness for forty years, surely He can take care of you and all your needs.

STUFFED BAKED POTATOES

8 medium white baking potatoes
1 cup skim milk, slitely heated
1 cup fat free mild Cheddar cheese, grated
8 ounce fat free margarine
pepper to taste
2 teaspoons chopped onion tops
6 slices turkey bacon, fried crisp and crumbled

METHOD:

Wash potatoes, wrap in foil - punch a few holes in each potato and bake at 450 degrees until potatoes are fully cooked.
About 2 hours.
Remove from oven, cut off slice from top of each potato and scoop out inside.
Mash well.
Add margarine, cheese, pepper and milk.
Mix thoroughly.
Add chopped onion tops and bacon and stir litely.
Fill scooped out shells with potato mixture and sprinkle more grated cheese on top of potato.
Bake in 350 degree oven for 15 to 20 minutes, or until cheese is melted and potatoes are hot.
This may be prepared ahead of time and baked to serve later.

SERVES: 8

FAT GRAMS PER SERVING:2

Nutritional Analysis Per Serving:

cal	*g. fat*	*(% of cal)*	*g.fib*	*mg. chol*	*mg. sod*
193	*2.09*	*10*	*2.57*	*10*	*462*

STUFFED ZUCCHINI

4 medium zucchini
1 pound package frozen corn
1 1/2 teaspoons seasoned salt
4 ounces fat free egg substitute
1 medium onion, chopped
1/4 cup grated fat free sharp Cheddar cheese

METHOD:

Scrub zucchini, cut off ends (do not pare).
Cook whole zucchini in boiling water (10 minutes).
Cool.
Cut zucchini in half, lengthwise.
With spoon carefully remove the fleshy part of zucchini from shells.
Chop the fleshy part into small pieces.
Combine corn, seasoned salt, fat free egg substitute and onion.
Pile mixture into zucchini shells.
Place in baking pan, sprinkle with grated cheese.
Bake uncovered in 350 degree oven for 30 minutes.

SERVES: 8

FAT GRAMS PER SERVING: 1

Nutritional Analysis Per Serving:

cal	g. fat	(%of cal)	g.fib	mg.chol	mg. sod
123	0.84	6	1.51	0.50	339

SUNDAY BLACK-EYED PEAS

2 cups black-eyed peas
4 slices turkey bacon, diced
1 medium onion, minced
1 teaspoon salt
1/8 teaspoon pepper
1 teaspoon dry mustard
1 teaspoon powder ginger
3/4 cup honey

METHOD:

Cover peas with water and cook on low overnight.
Fry bacon until crisp; discard fat.
Combine all ingredients in slow cooker.
Cook on low 8-9 hours.

SERVES: 8

FAT GRAMS PER SERVING: 2

Nutritional Analysis Per Serving:

cal	*g. fat*	*(% of cal)*	*g.fib*	*mg. chol*	*mg. sod*
264	*1.89*	*6*	*11.75*	*5*	*201*

SWEET POTATO DELITE

2 1/2 cups mashed, cooked sweet potatoes or yams (about 1 1/2 pounds)
3/4 cup lite brown sugar
1 tablespoon molasses
1 teaspoon cinnamon
1 teaspoon ginger
1/4 teaspoon nutmeg
4 ounces fat free egg substitute
Peel of 1/2 tangerine or orange, cut into thin julienne strips

METHOD:

In a bowl, combine all ingredients.
Place in well sprayed (lite cooking spray) cooker.
Cook on high 2-3 hours.
Remove from cooker.

SERVES: 6

FAT GRAMS PER SERVING: FAT FREE

Nutritional Analysis Per Serving:

cal	*g. fat*	*(%of cal)*	*g.fib*	*mg.chol*	*mg. sod*
326	*0.31*	*1*	*7.56*	*0.00*	*53*

SWEET POTATOES MARMALADE

3 15-ounce cans sweet potatoes, drained
4 ounces fat free margarine
3 tablespoons orange marmalade
1/2 cup Lite brown sugar
2 tablespoons grated orange rind
1 teaspoon salt

METHOD:

Combine margarine, orange marmalade, brown sugar, orange rind and salt in saucepan and simmer about 5 minutes, stirring frequently. Add drained potatoes and cook for 15 to 20 minutes until potatoes are well glazed.

SERVES: 10

FAT GRAMS PER SERVING: FAT FREE

Nutritional Analysis Per Serving:

cal	g. fat	(% of cal)	g.fib	mg. chol	mg. sod
209	0.39	2	3.91	0.00	144

TOMATO AND BEANS

1 1/2 cups great northern beans
2 medium onions, chopped
3 stalks celery, chopped
1/2 cup parsley, chopped
1 8-ounce can tomato sauce
1/2 teaspoon basil
4 tablespoons flour
4 tablespoons fat free margarine

METHOD:

Soak beans in water overnight.
Combine all ingredients except flour and margarine in cooker.
Add fresh water to cover.
Cook on low 10-12 hours, or on high 5-6 hours.
To thicken soup, remove 1/4 cup liquid and combine with flour and margarine.
Return mixture to cooker.

SERVES: 5

FAT GRAMS PER SERVING: 1

Nutritional Analysis Per Serving:

cal	*g. fat*	*(%of cal)*	*g.fib*	*mg.chol*	*mg. sod*
280	*1.04*	*3*	*3.56*	*0.00*	*660*

Yard Sale?

Every once in awhile, it is a good idea to have a yard sale.

To get rid of the stuff that you don't need, use or want anymore. You can be blessed by making some extra money and then benefit from the additional room.

We need to have a yard sale in our minds. We need to get rid of a lot of that old stuff. The Word says that we are to renew our minds. The Good Book also tells us to be careful when we clean house. We need to fill that empty space with godly things or the Word says that our house (mind) will be in worse shape than when we started.

It is like trying to get rid of a bad habit. You need to replace the bad habit with a good one or what you end up with may be worse than the first. Many quit smoking, but then start eating.

We need to renew the minds that grew up with worldly thinking, to godly thinking, so that we can have the mind of Christ.

TOMATO NONSTICK SKILLET CABBAGE

1 16-ounce can tomatoes
1 teaspoon instant beef bouillon
3 cups shredded cabbage

METHOD:

Drain the tomatoes, saving juice.
In medium Nonstick skillet heat juice from tomatoes and bouillon until bouillon is dissolved.
Stir in cabbage; cover litely and cook 3 minutes, stirring occasionally.
Add tomatoes; cover and cook until cabbage is crisp and tender and tomatoes are heated through (3 to 5 minutes).

SERVES: 4

FAT GRAMS PER SERVING: 1

Nutritional Analysis Per Serving:

cal	*g. fat*	*(%of cal)*	*g.fib*	*mg.chol*	*mg. sod*
64	*0.72*	*10*	*2.89*	*0.02*	*430*

VEGETABLE BEAN SOUP

1 pound dry navy beans
6 cups water
1 1/2 sliced carrots
1 28-ounce can tomatoes
1/4 teaspoon pepper
1 pound Mr. Turkey polish sausage
2 medium onions, sliced
2 stalks celery, in chunks
1 teaspoon Worcestershire sauce

METHOD:

Combine all ingredients and simmer covered for 3 to 3 1/2 hours.

SERVES: 8

FAT GRAMS PER SERVING: 2

Nutritional Analysis Per Serving:

cal	*g. fat*	*(% of cal)*	*g.fib*	*mg. chol*	*mg. sod*
271	*2.32*	*8*	*14.16*	*20*	*756*

VEGGIE STROGANOFF

1 tablespoon fat free margarine
1/3 cup finely chopped onion
1 clove garlic, minced
1 10 3/4-ounce can cream of mushroom soup
1 4-ounce can slice mushrooms, drained
2 tablespoons catsup
1 cup fat free sour cream

METHOD:

Combine margarine, onion and garlic in 2-quart casserole dish.
Cook, covered, on full power for 2 to 3 1/2 minutes, or until onion is tender.
Stir in soup, mushrooms and catsup.
Heat, covered, on full power for 1 1/2 to 3 1/2 minutes, or until heated through.
Stir in sour cream.
Heat, covered, on full power for 1 to 2 1/2 minutes, or until sour cream is heated through.
May be served over cooked noodles or rice.

SERVES: 4

FAT GRAMS PER SERVING: 6

Nutritional Analysis Per Serving:

cal	g. fat	(%of cal)	g.fib	mg.chol	mg. sod
187	6.03	29	1.09	9	963

YAMS

6 large yams
1/2 cup Lite brown sugar, firmly packed
1 tablespoon cornstarch
1/2 teaspoon cinnamon
1/4 teaspoon nutmeg
1 cup orange juice
2 tablespoons fat free margarine
1/2 teaspoon salt

METHOD:

Pierce skin of each yam several times with a fork or knife. Arrange yams on microwave-safe paper towel in oven, leaving about 1 inch in between each yam.
Cook on full power for 16 to 21 minutes, or until tender.
Turn yams over halfway through cooking time.
Let stand until cool enough to handle.
Combine brown sugar, cornstarch, cinnamon and nutmeg in 1-quart casserole dish.
Gradually stir in orange juice.
Cook, covered, on full power for 3 to 5 minutes, or until thickened and bubbling.
Stir 1 to 2 times during cooking time.
Stir margarine into sauce. Set aside.
Peel yams and cut in half lengthwise.
Place yams in 2-quart utility dish. Season with salt.
Pour sauce over yams.
Heat on full power for 2 1/2 to 4 1/2 minutes, or until heated through and bubbling.

SERVES: 12

FAT GRAMS PER SERVING: FAT FREE

Nutritional Analysis Per Serving:

cal	*g. fat*	*(% of cal)*	*g.fib*	*mg. chol*	*mg. sod*
214	*0.32*	*1*	*6.32*	*0.00*	*64*

ZIPPY GLAZED CARROTS

2 tablespoons fat free margarine
1/4 cup lite brown sugar
2 tablespoons prepared mustard
1/4 teaspoon salt
3 cups sliced carrots, cooked and drained
1 tablespoon chopped parsley

METHOD:

Melt margarine in nonstick skillet.
Stir in brown sugar, mustard and salt.
Add cooked carrots, heat.
Stir constantly for about 5 minutes until glazed.
Sprinkle with parsley.

SERVES: 6

FAT GRAMS PER SERVING: FAT FREE

Nutritional Analysis Per Serving:

cal	*g. fat*	*(%of cal)*	*g.fib*	*mg.chol*	*mg. sod*
53	*0.41*	*7*	*1.67*	*0.00*	*149*

Flat Tire

A flat tire is a real inconvenience.

If you are in a hurry, it can really get you upset. If you are on a trip and have every spare inch in the car filled with luggage, we are talking about a mess to get to the tire. However, most of us know what to do and we get it done and go on our way.

We get many flat tires in life. We shouldn't be surprised. The Good Book says that we will have trials and tests. Even if you buy new tires every six months, there can still be that nail in the road that you didn't see.

As Christians, we should know or learn how to take care of and get through the tests and trials that come in life.

We should use the Word of God, take care of the problem, and continue on the way. If you aren't sure how to do it, call for help. There are many people out there who have been through it before.

The Good Book is here to help you with the same comfort that they were helped with.

They are to pass it on.

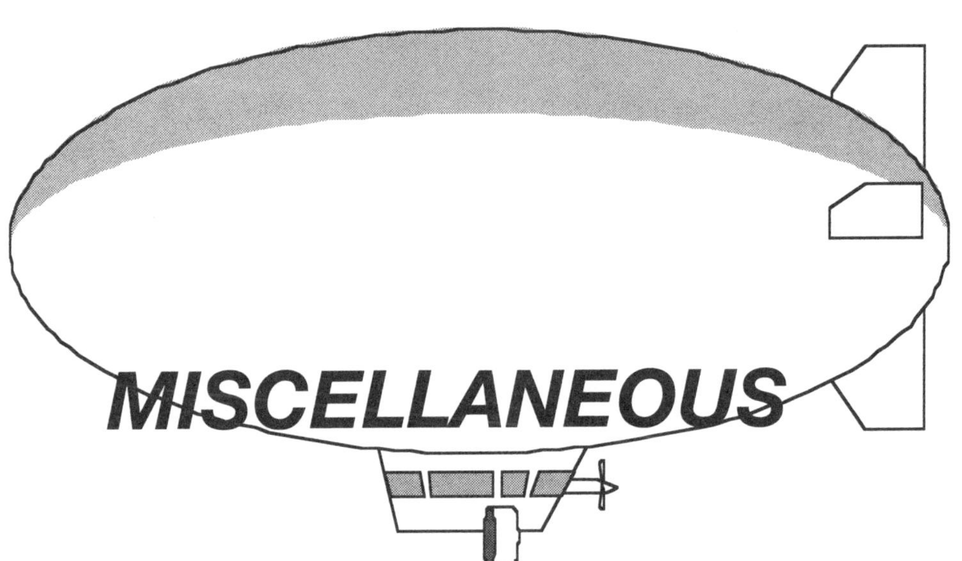
MISCELLANEOUS

INDEX TO MISC

CHEESE PUDDING

6 slices fat free toast
1/4 cup fat free margarine
2 1/2 cups fat free sliced American cheese
6 ounces fat free egg substitute
2 1/2 cups skim milk
1/4 teaspoon dry mustard

METHOD:

Butter toast, quarter each slice.
Alternate layers of bread and cheese in 2-quart oblong baking dish, with top layer cheese.
Combine fat free egg substitute, milk and seasonings.
Pour over all.
Bake in slow oven, 325 degrees, 30-45 minutes or until knife comes out clean.
If you wish, decorate after baking with drained, warmed canned asparagus.

SERVES: 6

FAT GRAMS PER SERVING: FAT FREE

NOTE: N. analysis does NOT include asparagus.

Nutritional Analysis Per Serving:

cal	*g. fat*	*(%of cal)*	*g.fib*	*mg.chol*	*mg. sod*
162	*0.19*	*1*	*2.00*	*8*	*778*

FISHERMAN'S TARTAR SAUCE

1 cup fat free mayonnaise
2 tablespoons kosher dill pickle, finely chopped
2 tablespoons onion, finely chopped
1 teaspoon lemon juice
Dash of pepper
1/4 cup fat free sour cream (optional)

METHOD:

Combine all ingredients well and chill.

SERVES: 10

FAT GRAMS PER SERVING: FAT FREE

Nutritional Analysis Per Serving:

cal	*g. fat*	*(% of cal)*	*g.fib*	*mg. chol*	*mg. sod*
28	*0.02*	*1*	*0.03*	*0.80*	*229*

FRUIT OMELET (MICROWAVE)

1 slice turkey bacon
1 small apple or pear, sliced (about 3/4 cup)
1 teaspoon fat free margarine
1 teaspoon Lite brown sugar
Dash of cinnamon
6 ounces Egg Beaters
2 tablespoons skim milk
1/2 teaspoon cinnamon-sugar

METHOD:

Layer turkey bacon between paper towels in 9-inch microwave safe plate.
Microwave (high) 1 to 1 1/2 minutes or until turkey bacon is crisp; set aside.
Wipe excess drippings from pie plate with paper towels.
Combine apple, margarine, brown sugar and cinnamon in small microwave-safe bowl.
Microwave (high) uncovered 2 1/2 to 3 minutes or until tender, stirring once. Set aside.
Beat together eggs and milk. Pour into pie plate. Cover with plastic wrap. Microwave (high) 1 to 1 1/2 minutes or until edges start to set.
Microwave (high) 1 1/2 to 2 1/2 minutes or until egg is just about set.
Spoon apple mixture and crumbled turkey bacon over half the omelet.
Fold over other half and slide out of pie plate onto serving plate.
If egg is still soft, microwave 15 to 30 seconds or until set. Sprinkle with cinnamon-sugar.

SERVES: 1

FAT GRAMS PER SERVING: 3

Nutritional Analysis Per Serving:

cal	*g. fat*	*(%of cal)*	*g.fib*	*mg.chol*	*mg. sod*
180	*2.85*	*14*	*2.13*	*11*	*477*

MILK GRAVY FOR BREAKFAST

1 tablespoon turkey sausage meat drippings
3 tablespoon fat free margarine
2 tablespoon flour
1 1/2 cups evaporated skim milk

METHOD:

Heat meat drippings in iron skillet.
Add margarine, stir until brown
Stir in flour untill brown.
Slowly add milk untill desired thickness.
Salt and pepper to taste.

SERVES: 4

FAT GRAMS PER SERVING: 3

Nutritional Analysis Per Serving:

cal	*g. fat*	*(% of cal)*	*g.fib*	*mg. chol*	*mg. sod*
121	*3.43*	*25*	*0.10*	*7*	*178*

STEWED APPLES

6 medium apples, cored and peeled about 1 inch down
1/2 cup sugar
2 tablespoons raisins
1 teaspoon cinnamon
2 tablespoons fat free margarine
1/2 cup water

METHOD:

Mix sugar, raisins and cinnamon.
Stuff apples with sugar mixture and dot them with margarine.
Pour water into cooker.
Add apples.
Cook on low 7-8 hours.

SERVES: 6

FAT GRAMS PER SERVING: 1

Nutritional Analysis Per Serving:

cal	*g. fat*	*(%of cal)*	*g.fib*	*mg.chol*	*mg. sod*
112	*0.51*	*4*	*3.64*	*0.00*	*31*

SWEET AND SOUR SAUCE

1/2 cup honey
1 tablespoon cornstarch
1/3 cup red wine vinegar
1/3 cup fat free chicken broth
1/4 cup finely chopped bell pepper
2 tablespoons chopped pimento
1 tablespoon soy sauce
1/4 teaspoon garlic powder
1/4 teaspoon ground ginger

METHOD:

In a saucepan, combine honey and cornstarch.
Stir in vinegar, chicken broth, bell pepper, pimento, soy sauce, garlic powder and ginger.
Cook and stir until thickened and bubbly.
Serve hot with meat or poultry.

SERVES: 6

FAT GRAMS PER SERVING: FAT FREE

Nutritional Analysis Per Serving:

cal	*g. fat*	*(% of cal)*	*g.fib*	*mg. chol*	*mg. sod*
109	*0.03*	*0.00*	*0.20*	*0.00*	*564*

CARROT OR SQUASH SOUFFLE

2 tablespoons fat free margarine
2 tablespoons flour
1/2 cup skim milk
1/2 teaspoon salt
1 1/2 cups mashed carrots (or squash)
8 ounces egg substitute

METHOD:

Melt margarine, add flour and stir until well blended.
Add milk and cook until thick.
Remove from fire and add salt and beaten egg substitute.
Fold in mashed carrots.
Pour into well sprayed ring mold or baking dish.
Set in pan of hot water and bake 1 hour in moderate oven and serve at once.

SERVES: 4

FAT GRAMS PER SERVING: 1

Nutritional Analysis Per Serving:

cal	g. fat	(%of cal)	g.fib	mg.chol	mg. sod
346	1.49	4	7.10	1	470

VEGETABLE CASSEROLE

6 slices skinless white meat turkey, cut up
1 pound ground turkey breast
2 large onions, chopped
1 16-ounce can pork & beans
1 pound can stewed tomatoes
3/4 cup Lite brown sugar
Chili powder to taste

METHOD:

Place all ingredients in a large casserole dish and bake 3 hours at 300 degrees or until meat is done.

SERVES: 6

FAT GRAMS PER SERVING: 2

Nutritional Analysis Per Serving:

cal	*g. fat*	*(% of cal)*	*g.fib*	*mg. chol*	*mg. sod*
301	*1.98*	*6*	*8.58*	*19*	*1074*

TWICE-BAKED POTATOES

4 medium (7 ounce each) baking potatoes
1/2 cup fat free sour cream
1 (3 ounce) package fat free cream cheese softened
2 tablespoons fat free margarine
1/2 teaspoon garlic or onion salt
1 teaspoon snipped chives
1/8 teaspoon pepper
1/4 cup shredded Cheddar fat free cheese

METHOD:

Pierce skins of potatoes with fork.
Arrange potatoes on microwave-safe paper towel in oven.
Cook on full power for 10 to 14 minutes, or until potatoes are done.
Turn potatoe over halfway through cooking time.
Cut slice from top of each potato and scoop out insides into mixing bowl.
Add remaining ingredients, except Cheddar cheese.
Beat until smooth.
Spoon back into potato shells.
Arrange stuffed potatoes on serving plate.
Heat on full power for 1 1/2 to 3 minutes ,or until potatoes are heated through.
Top potatoes with cheese.
Let stand until cheese begins to melt.

SERVES: 4

FAT GRAMS PER SERVING: FAT FREE

Nutritional Analysis Per Serving:

cal	*g. fat*	*(%of cal)*	*g.fib*	*mg.chol*	*mg. sod*
234	*0.21*	*1*	*3.38*	*8*	*239*

TAMALE CASSEROLE

1	pound ground lean sirloin
1/2	cup chopped onion
1/2	cup chopped green bell peppers
1	package chili seasoning mix
1	pound fresh tomatoes
12	ounces whole kernel corn, frozen
1	cup (12 ounces) yellow cornmeal
2 1/2	cups cold water
1	cup Cheddar cheese, fat free

METHOD:

Brown ground meat in a skillet until crumbly; drain fat, pat dry.
Add onion, green peppers, seasoning mix and tomatoes; combine thoroughly.
Bring mixture to a boil; reduce heat and simmer, uncovered, ten minutes.
Meanwhile, combine cornmeal, water; cook until thick, about 15 minutes.
Add corn to beef mixture.
Spread mixture in a 2-quart oblong baking dish.
Spread cooked cornmeal evenly over beef mixture.
Bake in preheated 350 degrees oven 40 minutes.
Sprinkle grated cheese over top; bake 5 minutes longer.

SERVES: 8

FAT GRAMS PER SERVING: 3

Nutritional Analysis Per Serving:

cal	*g. fat*	*(% of cal)*	*g.fib*	*mg. chol*	*mg. sod*
247	*2.91*	*11*	*1.42*	*28*	*439*

CONCLUSION:

Well. Here we are at the end of the journey.
However, when you walk through one door and leave that space you also enter another “world” or space. This may be the start of the a new one for you, a new healthier you.
You have the makings of a program for yourself.
Experience some of the joys of low-fat cooking.
Relax.
In fact you may wonder whether or not it is really you.
I heard about one such incident as well as many such experiences in my own life.

CAN THAT BE ME?

As I passed by a window, I saw a reflection. The person looking back at me was somehow familiar, and I wondered who she was.

As I took another look, I realized that the person I was looking at was me. But wait -- there’s something missing -- there’s less of me.

There was a time when I’d walk by windows and mirrors quickly, not wanting to see my reflection. The image was one I disliked, and I’d tell myself I had to do something about it -- but I never did.

Yet this new reflection now tells me, “stop and look -- you’ve finally done it.” I’ve won -- that’s really me!

You can keep yourself in reasonable good health and keep a high energy level too.

DAILY LIVING
"GOING DEEPER" SECTION

Note: All references are from the English Bible (Old and New Testaments). A good concordance and a readable translation can enhance your walk for a deeper spirituality. -f.r.-

25 HOUR A DAY?

Proverbs 4:23 Matthew 5:8
Matthew 15:18-20

A FATHER'S LOVE

John 10:17 1 John 4:11
1 John 2:13,14

ADDICTION

Revelation 21:8,27
Matthew 7:5

AGE

Psalm 71: 9,18
Psalm 148: 12

AIR CONDITION?

Psalms 28:7
Isaiah 12:2

ATTIDUDE?

Proverbs 10:12
Mark 12:30,31
Romans 5:8

BANK

Matthew 6:19-21

CAN'T DO ANYMORE?

Matthew 11:28-30
Matthew 25:15

CASH A CHECK

John 10:10 2 Peter 1:3
Romans 10:17

CHRISTMAS

Psalms 9:12 Psalms 103:2
Deuteronomy 4:9

COOKIES AND ICE CREAM

Romans 12: 1-3
Ephesians 4:23

COUCH POTATO?

Hebrews 4:12
1 Corinthians 15:58
James 2:24

DID YOU EVER PLANT A SHADE TREE?

Psalms 1:3 Psalms 11:30
Luke 6:44

EMPTY FEELINGS?

Psalm 23 John 10:1-16
John 15:11

FALL

Romans 8:28-29

FAMILY

Luke 8: 19-21
Ephesians 3:15

FANTASY

Deuteronomy 30:19
Isaiah 26:3 Mark 12:30

FAST FOOD

2 Peter 3:8-10

FEAR

2 Timothy 1:7 Isaiah 41:10
Psalms 118:6

FIFTY PERCENT

2 Timothy 1:7 Isaiah 41:10
Psalms 118:6

FLAT TIRE

2 Corinthians 1:4

GIVE THANKS

Psalms 28:7; 104:1
Philippians 4:6
Colossians 2:7

GOOD BOOKS?

2 Timothy 3:16,17

GOT A PROBLEM?

2 Corinthians 1:3,4 and
12:8,9
Proverbs 3:5,6 Psalms 37:5

HOLIDAY SEASON

Ecclesiastes 3:1-8
Hebrews 4:16

HOW DO YOU CAST YOUR BURDENS?

I Peter 5:7 John 21:5-6
John 16:24

HURT FEELINGS?

Matthew 18:22 Luke 6:27-28
Proverbs 2 Psalms 103:12

IF LOOKS COULD?

James chapter 2
Colossians 1:16
Titus 3:8

IS BIG BETTER?

Philippians 3:3

IT'S HARD

James 1:2,12

JOY OF A CHILD, THE

John 15:13 Matthew 9:37
Matthew 18:3

KIDS

Psalms 127:3 Proverbs 17:6

LIKE A CHILD

Matthew 18:1-6
Hebrews 6:18 Matthew 6:33
John 3:16 I John 4:4
Romans 8:28 Proverbs 18:10
John 10:4 Matthew 6:8

LIKED

Matthew 6:25-27

LOOK FOR THE GOOD

Romans 4:20, 21 and 8:28-30
Hebrews 11:1,6
Matthew 7:1-5

LOOKING FOR SOMETHING TO DO??

James 1:27 Matthew 25:35

LOVE IS STILL WORKING

1 Corinthians 13:13
Proverbs 10:12
Isaiah 41:10
Matthew 22:37-43

MONDAYS

Psalms 100:4

MOTHERS

Proverbs 31
Proverbs 30:11
Ephesians 6:2

MY JOB

Matthew 6:28-34

NEED A FRIEND?

Gen 8:22 II Corinthians 9:6
Galatians 6:7
II Corinthians 1:4

"NO"

Romans 13:10 1John 4:18

PIZZA?

Psalms 133:1

RECEIVE

Acts 20: 35
Hebrews 10:36 1 Peter 1:9

REJECTION???

Hosea 4:6 Isaiah 53:3
Luke 9:22

RELAX

Matthew 6:33,34 Psalms 23

RICH/POOR?

Matthew 5:3
1 Timothy 6:17-19

SNACKS

Matthew 4:4

SUGAR OR...

1 Corinthians 13:13
Johnn 3:16
Proverbs 16:24
Psalms 104:34

SUPER GLUE?

Romans 8:38-39

USELESS

Isaiah 55:11
2 Peter 1:3

YARD SALE

Matthew 12: 43-45

THERE'S NO EXPENSIVE CLINIC, NO SPECIAL PRODUCTS TO BUY, NO DRASTIC CHANGES TO MAKE, NO COMMERCIAL DIET PROGRAMS...

ITS WEIGHT-LOSS WITH A DOWN HOME SOUTHERN FLAIR

She's called the **First Lady of Homestyle Cooking** by followers. She appeals to the ordinary person wanting to lose weight with ordinary home-style cooking. And there must be a lot of ordinary people out there because Natoma Riley has sold **thousands** of copies of **Natoma's Low Fat Home-Style Cooking** since it first was published not quite a year ago.

Maybe it's the absence of slick marketeering or the fact that her menus are based on "good common sense" that endears her to the thousands who have purchased her book or those that sign up for her menus at her company, the Low Fat Connection.

After all, she was just a working mother with three children and the wife of a minister before it all began. When she busted a zipper trying to squeeze her 253 pound frame into a size 22 pair of jeans eight years ago it marked the end of her fat life and the start toward a thin one. But, being a Southern Indiana girl who grew up on chicken and cornbread, Natoma didn't want to give up the foods she loved. "I would go to bed crying I was so hungry," says Natoma. So she embarked on a mission to de-fat her favorite foods and the result of that research was a loss of 110 pounds in 14 months. Eight years later she's still slim and has written a cookbook fitted with homestyle recipes and homespun flavor.

Index

D

INVITE ME TO YOUR WORK PLACE!

MOST POPULAR TOPICS

IMPROVING PERSONAL BUSINESS PRODUCTIVITY WITH LOW-FAT LIFESTYLE.
The better you look and feel, the better you will do in your business. Here's a practical, step-by-step; here's how to look as slim as you want, radiate vitality and never go hungry.

IMPROVING EMPLOYEE PRODUCTIVITY WITH LOW-FAT DIETS.
Slimmer employees are happier, healthier, friendlier, have higher self-esteem, and they work harder. Here's how to add a low-fat weight-loss program to your business.

SLEEKER SALESPEOPLE ARE BETTER SALESPEOPLE.
Want your salespeople to make more sales calls? Want them to like each other, customers and themselves more? Help them lose weight with 10 easy steps.

FOR BOOKING INFORMATION, OR A LIST OF ADDITIONAL SEMINARS, SPEECHES OR PRESENTATIONS CONTACT:

Other Natoma Products

Natoma's Deluxe Menu Kit

- Natoma's Deluxe Menu
  - 28 day menu plan.
  - Plus, recipes from Natoma's Low Fat Homestyle Cookbook.

- Natoma The First Lady of Homestyle Cooking Video
  - Natoma answers the most often asked questions regarding her weight loss plan, and shares secrets of her permanent weight loss.
- Natoma's Realistic Guide to Weight Loss Video
  - Natoma gives a step by step explanation of the 28 day menu plan.
- Fatbusting Your Way to Better Health
  - Basic fatbusting tips.

Natoma's Low Fat Homestyle Cookbook

- Low Fat Recipes of your favorite Homestyle Meals

Natoma's The First Lady of Homestyle Cooking Video

Natoma's First Lady Combo Pack

- Natoma The First Lady of Homestyle Cooking Video
- Natoma's Low Fat Homestyle Cookbook

To Order Now Call 1-800-343-8101

Watch for Natoma's next book in early 1996